THAT BLACK HASIDIC LADY

A Memoir of a Dark-Skinned Hasidic Lady

Sara Braun

Copyright © 2023 by Sade Coppens

All rights reserved, including the right to reproduce this book or portions thereof in any form whatsoever. For information, contact teamsarabraun@gmail.com or 845-545-3379

All photographs courtesy of the author.

For information about special discounts for bulk purchases, contact teamsarabraun@gmail.com or 845-545-3379

For information about live events or speaking engagements, Please contact teamsarabraun@gmail.com or 845-545-3379

ISBN 978-4477-7482-2

ISBN 978-1-4478-0041-5 e-book

The names and identifying characteristics of everyone in this book have been changed. While all the incidents described in this book are true, certain events may have been curtailed to protect the privacy and identity of the individuals involved, and a very small number of events may not be in the exact order in which they occurred to ensure continuity of the narrative. All scenes and dialogue were rendered as closely as possible to actual conversations that took place, to the best of the author's recollection.

TABLE OF CONTENTS

My Family --- 1
Alisa --- 27
March 3, 2004 --- 34
Au-Pair for Family Scheutema --- 47
Family Jansen --- 51
Yitzchak --- 61
Being black and Hasidic --- 68
Henya Lederman --- 71
Moving to Brooklyn --- 75
The Gestetners --- 84
My infamous friends --- 91
The other side of a perfect orthodox father. --- 101
Devorah --- 105
Ari Glick --- 120
Challenges in being black and Jewish --- 126
The Rebbeshe chasuna --- 136
Going upstate for the first time --- 151
Ski trip to Vermont --- 169
My wedding --- 181
Married life --- 215
Bubbe Glick --- 223
The birth of my first child --- 232
The birth of my second child --- 247
Back to New York --- 270
Conclusion --- 277

THAT BLACK HASIDIC LADY

My Family

Wow! Just like in magazines! This place is full of energy and different kinds of cultures. Everyone seems to have a solid purpose. They are always laser-focused as they are doing something or on their way to somewhere without looking left or right. I just love this place called New York City!

I was thirteen years old, and my family and I were on vacation in New York.

"Mama?! I am so going to live in this city. When I am 18 years old, I will move from the Netherlands to New York!" I said.

My mother looked at me with a small polite smile, yet the word "whatever" was written across her forehead. She responded, "All right. That's great, honey."

My mother Gita. The bearer of this black Jewish, creative, free-spirited, opera singing, gardening loving, vegetarian, affectionate, typical Pisces, and "complicated" me today. Me. The *Heimishe* dark colored Jewish woman who was born and raised in Europe, with strong Hasidic roots and yet from a non-Jewish father. I have always been extremely close to my mother, so close that we often shared telepathic experiences. They say that I look just like her. My brothers often mistakenly said "Hi mama" when I was a teenager as they walked into the house. A few times, I have caught myself taking a few steps towards my own reflection in the mirrors of department stores while searching for my mother, who was endlessly looking at shoes.

I have always had the utmost respect for my mother. Many of my friends would say "My mother said this and my mother said that but I am not listening to her!" I just could not understand this because to me, my mother was the coolest most wonderful person alive who had the right answer to everything. I always figured that other girls felt the same way about their mothers. "How am I not going to listen to my mother?" I would think. My mother knew everything!

She always looked so very elegant to me in a way that made me feel uncomfortable for her. She was always in high heels with her hair perfectly done. For as long as I can remember, I knew I would never be like my mother. She is so gorgeous, graceful, and flawless. I was a tomboy as a child. I was constantly on the go, assertive, quick, no filter, and both physically and mentally strong. I enjoyed playing outside with the neighborhood children sometimes, pretending to cook for our baby dolls as we played around in the grass and the soil. I would get dirty, but I didn't care. All of a sudden, I would hear my mother approaching in the far distance. I would first hear her heels on the concrete "click clack click clack". She had this easy-steady walk, almost as if her heels magically carried her to the beat of the Bee Gees's song "Night Fever," as if she had all the time in the world. No one besides my mother walked like that in my world. I would search for her immediately. Where did those footsteps come from? My head would go in all directions. Of course, she had already spotted me. And there she was with a broad smile on her face, fancy, in stiff clothing and itchy panty-hosed legs, and in 6-inch heels.

To me, that daily image of my approaching mother was the epitome of a perfect woman. Though she was not necessarily a perfect traditional mother, because in my mind, perfect traditional mothers wore their hair in a braid, a ponytail, or down if it was short. Perfect mothers dressed comfortably, drank coffee, and rode their bikes to wherever they needed to go. That was a typical Dutch mother in my rural Dutch community. My mother did not do any of that. In my mind, I felt far from the woman my mother was. Yet, with all that perfection, I was very aware that she loved imperfect me more than she loved her own perfect self.

I grew up in an area called De Beemster in the Netherlands with my parents, my sister Miriam, and my two older brothers Robert and Levi. I was the youngest and a typical rather spoiled youngest daughter. I was very intuitive and had a strong will. My sister Miriam is eight years older than me and is quite the opposite of me. We rarely interacted or even spoke with each other because of our incompatible personalities. Miriam was very reserved, quiet and kept to herself in her room, yet stubborn and very greedy as a child. She would just "go with the flow" all the time and I just did not get that. I would question or challenge anyone at any time if I felt that something did not add up or felt unjustified. I would challenge her a lot as well, simply to shake-up her simple, slow-moving energy a bit. She never liked it of course.

My brother Robert is three years older than I am. He too preferred to keep to himself, but at least he got out there every now and then. He preferred to play alone and had a hard time sharing as a child. He would knock me over mercilessly if I dared to mess with his Lego creations. Even so, I could never resist, and took a punch if I had to.

My other brother Levi is two years older than me. He was the cool one. He was very popular in the neighborhood. He was smart, quick, witty, ambitious, and a leader in everything he did. Among the older kids, my name was not "Sara"; it was "Levi's sister". He was popular and well respected and I tried to hang out with him and his friends a lot but I was not always welcome. They moved quickly and often ventured out of the village, much further than I was allowed. They often did not have time for me. I was the closest to Levi though. He loved a challenge and I could relate to his actions, his sense of witty humor and outgoing nature.

Our neighborhood was safe and pleasant. We lived in a small and tight community where everyone knew each other. All children attended the same school, and there were always children playing outside. My fantasies grew wild outside. I was always pretending that I was a grown-up running a household with a gazillion children. I had dolls or my friends' younger siblings as my children, my brother's go-cart as my car, grass and weeds as vegetables, soil as stamppot (Dutch potato dish), and old pots and pans to cook with. I love animals. We had chickens, roosters, bunnies, Guinea pigs, and I helped on a local farm over the weekends as well. I was a very happy child with big imaginations.

My father was a musician. He was quite popular among his fellow South Americans. I always found his music to be enjoyable but intense. I could never relate to the type of dancing people did to his music. I found it quite wild and vulgar. I was never close to my father and never felt any type of connection really. I always felt that his morals and standards were flat-out weird and ungrounded. His sense of humor was puzzling to me, and it was as if we lived in two completely different worlds. His talking was always with such passion that I took it as him being ticked off by something. It made me feel like he was just never happy and was not in control of his emotions or something.

I found my father to be very demanding and stern; however, it was in such a way that it really did not leave any room for me to have my own opinions, wants or needs. I did not respect him as much as I respected my mother. He was a big bully, but despite this, I never feared him. I always found him rather weird and sad. Since I never really paid attention to him and often doubted him or didn't always follow through with his demands, I believe he disliked me as well.

My father complained often to my mother about me, but my mother understood where I was coming from. My sister Miriam was his perfectly reserved and obedient daughter. I must say that he did value family tremendously. He was an amazing cook and threw the most memorable neighborhood barbecues and birthday parties. Even at the beach he managed to get everyone to hang around our tent. He was a true natural at entertaining, and he was very welcoming to guests. One of my cousins even calls him "Papa" ever since he can remember because he lived more in our house than in his own house and my father treated him like his son.

In De Beemster, I attended a typical Dutch Montessori school. In addition to studying math, reading, and writing, we studied nature, the four seasons, different kinds of trees, birds, and butterflies, as well as their characteristics. We studied topics such as: What happens in autumn? Why do leaves fall off trees? What leaves belong to what tree? What tree attracts what type of insects and birds and why? Then we would go outside to collect the most beautiful orange-golden leaves that had fallen from the trees for our creative arts and crafts projects.

At the age of six, I learned how to sew, knit and do embroidery. It was mandatory for the students to study a different animal each month, write a whole report on it, and do a presentation about the animal for the class. With approximately 30 children in each class, your knowledge of animals becomes vast. Since we had quite a few animals at home, my first few book reports were always about the pets I owned. This way I could bring them to school as well.

Our family was one of the only colored families in our small Dutch village. Everybody knew us. We were "the exotic family" who knew how to cook delicious South American dishes full of flavor. Our skin color was just beautiful and we were so lucky to be sun-resistant. Even with sunscreen on, my friends would burn terribly in the summer if they weren't careful. In contrast, my siblings and I could just play endlessly in the beaming sun throughout the summer with only one application of sunscreen.

"I wish I had your hair. If you make a braid, you don't need to tie it at the end!" "There is so much you can do with your hair!" "My hair is so boring." These are the comments my friends often made about my hair. I, on the other hand, was always thinking, "I wish I had your hair because it's so simple in a ponytail without the need for any smelly and greasy frizz-taming hair products." My natural hair is very curly, and if I don't use anything to tame it, it gets very frizzy. My mother used to lather my hair with all sorts of hair lotions with strong, supposedly "delicious" scents. I could not stand the feel and smell of these hair products and still today I am very sensitive to scented hair products and the feel of greasy hair. My hair was beautiful and thick. In the summer it would get a reddish glow. When this happened, I felt that my hair looked dirty. It was as if I had stuck my hair in the mud or something, but I was never allowed to do anything about it.

Many of my friends adored my older brothers, especially Levi. Typical Dutch blonde boys were considered to be boring. My brothers were considered attractive, handsome and exotic. We were Jewish. Nobody in our town knew that we were Jewish because for one, we did not practice Judaism and furthermore, where I am from, you could not just tell everyone and anyone that you are Jewish. In the early nineties, people still tended to be quite shamelessly verbal about their negative impressions of Jews. We were still often considered to be those people who are inferior, "Hebrews," depressing, dirty and unsightly. Jews are not considered to be Caucasian either where I grew up and were not treated the same.

    We used cuss words in my youth with the word "Jew" in them, such as bum-Jew and dirty-Jew, and if you said or did something stupid, you could simply have been called a "Jew," as if the Jews invented stupid things. This was so normal that as a child, I did not even realize that these cuss words were related to the Jewish people. They pretty much sounded like one word to me. "Bum-Jew" sounded like "Bumjoo" to me; I never realized what it really meant. The fact that we were colored was just great, but being Jewish was a whole different, not-so-great story. You could not just proudly say that you are Jewish; you would be stigmatized instantly. I did not mind this. I grew up with the notion that Christmas was elegant, grand and for "normal" people, and Hanukkah was for weird low-life outsiders. Hanukkah was far less fun, and an alternative for those who do not deserve Christmas.

During my school years, we observed, celebrated, and honored Christmas, and it was always so beautiful. Nobody ever paid any attention to the Jewish Holiday Hanukkah in my village. Nobody cared. I had one other Jewish boy in my class. His family was openly Jewish. His name was Ezra and he was bullied mercilessly, so much so that he wet his pants all the time. His short and overweight mother with very pale skin, ice-blue eyes, and dark curly and frizzy hair would often come to school upset about something that had happened again.

My family did not practice Judaism. My father is not Jewish and my mother was discriminated so terribly by her lighter-skinned Jewish family that she does not want anything to do with it. My dear mother, so strong and stoic, yet sometimes if she talks about certain subjects, you can hear a hint of pain in her voice. My mother was the ever-elegant beauty of the neighborhood. She is stylish, can see through everything and everyone, and she has impeccable common sense.

My mother was born in a small country in the Northern part of South-America. She was raised by her mother, my grandmother, for the first five years of her life, together with her younger sister. My maternal grandmother was a simple woman. She was tall and striking with European-like slender features. However, unlike her mother and siblings, my grandmother had a dark complexion, and because of this, she was given away at birth to her father's side of the family. There was no room for a dark-skinned baby in my great-grandmother's perfect Jewish family where the majority was fair skinned with light colored eyes. My great-grandmother's husband at that time was partially black, but he came from a family who had a successful butcher business. He was rich, which made him acceptable.

My maternal grandfather was a "big *macher*" (A bigshot). He was also very tall and always wore a suit. There was a game show on television at that time that tested people's intelligence. My grandfather was the highest scoring competitor in the country and became quite famous and rich because of it. He was a ladies' man and he got to know my grandmother when she was his housekeeper. I remember the last time I saw my grandfather. He was old and not doing too well. In his stylish camel-brown suit, he sat in a chair on his birthday. He seemed too tall for this chair. His long legs made too much and too high of a bend at the knees and stretched too far out in my eyes. The same was true of his elbows. All he could do was sit. Despite his poor health, he was wearing his suit and carried tremendous pride.

My mother had a simple and happy upbringing up to the age of five. Her mother was a simple housekeeper. She led a simple and content life. They were poor, but with my grandmother's creativity, she was often able to provide my mother and her younger sister with beautiful hand-made dresses, delicious home-made treats, and the most fun and creative experiences. When my grandmother was 32, she stepped on a rusty nail outside her house. The rust entered her bloodstream and she slowly died of blood poisoning when my mother was only five years old.

While my grandmother was sick, her neighbors contacted my great-grandmother to deliver the news. The same great-grandmother who gave her daughter away 32 years ago rushed to my grandmother's bedside to take her back to her house and claim custody of my mother and her younger sister. My sick grandmother was put in a bed in the attic of her mother's house. Nobody was allowed to go up there to see her but my mother would visit her whenever she saw a chance. My grandmother was lying there on her back alone in a bed, with her face turned to the wall. My five-year-old mother would talk to her but my grandmother was unable to turn her head to face her daughter or even say anything back. All she could do was moan in a weak tone.

When my grandmother passed away, my mother was not informed of this sad news. She did not realize in her five-year-old mind that her mother had died. The bed in the attic was all of a sudden empty and my mother was waiting by the garden gate for her mother to return from wherever she was. All of a sudden, the song "Hey Jude" from the Beatles played on someone's radio and something clicked in my five-year-old mother's head. At that moment she realized that her mother would never return.

My great-grandmother got custody of my mother and aunt, and then my mother was further raised by my great-grandmother. My great-grandmother Greta was a German Jewish woman with dark hair and grey-green eyes. Her father was from Germany and her mother was from Belz, Galicia, Eastern Europe. They traveled to South America for business. South America had plantations, and with its conducive climate, the plantations produced an abundance of different kinds of highly sought-after spices and food.

My great-grandmother's face always reminded me of the face of that octopus witch from the Disney cartoon "Little Mermaid." As a child, I was never comfortable with her. She was a racist and raised her children to be racists as well. Some of her children were smarter and realized in their adult years that it was wrong to be racist. I remember how my great-grandmother forbade me to play with my light-skinned cousin's toys. "They are his toys!" she said. One day she forbade my mother to bring us to her birthday celebration because we were dark-skinned. This was the last straw for my mother and she broke contact with her grandmother. All her life my mother was treated differently by her grandmother and her aunts. My mother, despite her pride and beautiful features that were constantly complimented by others, was treated inferiorly by her own family because of the color of her skin.

My mother slept in the room in the attic where her mother passed away. While the rest of her family was not comfortable walking up there, my mother felt warm and safe in this room. It was as if her mother was there with her and comforted her. Despite the abuse she received from her family, my mother was a proud young lady with great self-respect. She turned simple shapeless school uniforms into perfectly fitted suits that looked like they came off the racks of 5th Avenue department stores. She enjoyed wearing high heels from a young age. If her grandmother asked her why in this world she was wearing high heels, my mother would respond that she wears high heels because it makes her feel "higher." Her response always upset her grandmother. She would yell, "What do you mean by higher? You are black! You are not high! Take them off!"

My mother was and is still stubborn. Nothing could break her. When my mother was fourteen years old, she secretly started dating another teenager of color. When my great-grandmother found out, she immediately made plans to send my mother to Europe to live with one of her daughters. My mother was not to date someone who was not Jewish, and on top of that, black.

One morning like all other mornings, my mother was told that she was leaving for the Netherlands the following day. Of course, my mother was devastated. She lived with her aunt in the Netherlands where she lived like some sort of Cinderella, complete with mean stepsisters, who were her own cousins. When my mother was sixteen, she met my father at a party. My father is also from South America. He was a famous musician. My mother was not interested in my father; however, my father had an abundance of wealth, and with bribes, he was able to persuade my great-grandmother to convince my mother to be with him.

My sister Miriam was born when my mother was nineteen, followed by my two brothers and me. When my second brother was born, my mother was already in a place of wanting to separate from my father. My mother definitely did not want to have more children with my father, but she got pregnant with me. My mother was so devastated that she considered an abortion. She drove to the clinic to have me aborted. However, as soon as she saw me moving around on the doctor's computer screen, she completely changed her mind, and here I am.

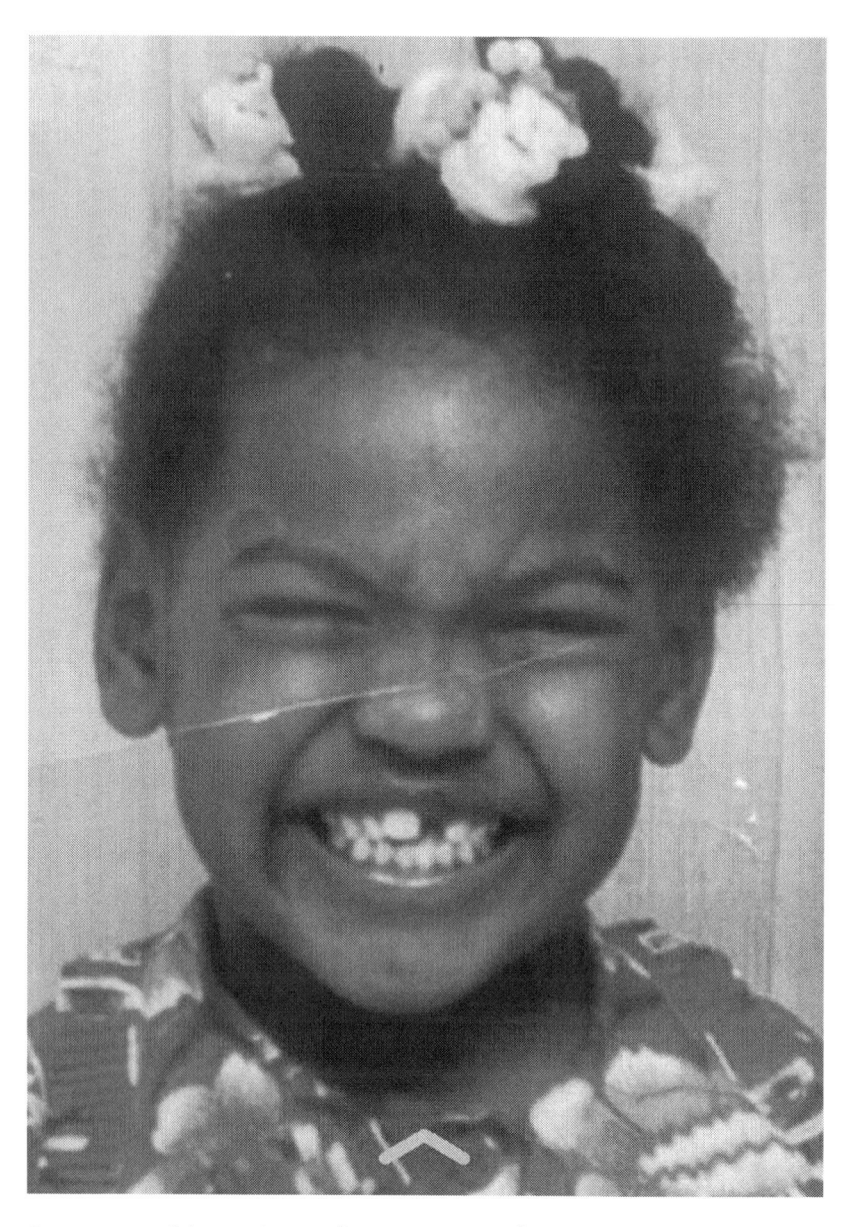

Four-year old me. According to my mother, I did not want to comb my hair this day and refused to smile for the picture. After my mother's and the photographer's constant pleading, I decided to smile like this.

I was born on March 3, 1986. My maternal grandmother was born on March 2, 1932. It was said by spiritual people that I was a gift from my grandmother to my mother, and other similar presumptions have been made throughout my life. I am named after my grandmother, Sara-Raizel. A few times I have had indescribable supernatural experiences which make me believe that I am strongly connected to my grandmother, who I have never met in my life because she passed away when my mother was only five years old.

I've always had a picture of my grandmother in my dining room. Every time I look at her face in that picture, there is a different expression in her face, depending on what runs through my head while looking at her picture. One time I was standing in front of the mirror detangling my wet hair when I saw my face clearly changing into hers. Even my skin color changed to hers for a few seconds. I almost fainted and was overcome by emotions. I was told that she lives inside me, and I do believe that.

I came into this world unexpectedly. All of a sudden, moments after my mother's first sign of labor, my head was lying between her legs with the nurses unprepared and unsterilized to receive me. Here I was, a chubby baby with a head full of hair. The day I was born I looked around at everyone one by one, according to my mother. I was instantly attached to my mother. She could not put me down or I would scream. Not even my father could hold me without me screaming. This insulted him tremendously and it was the beginning of a battle for my mother between him and myself. I rejected my father. This made him argue about me all the time with my mother. He did not like how she took me everywhere she went, and he did not want me to sleep in her bed. Every sign of love and affection my mother had for me, my father was arguing about me being spoiled.

My father found me to be spoiled and arrogant. Sometimes in the middle of the night when he came home from his performing gig, he would take me out of my mother's bed. He would then put me in my own bed. But before he put me in my own bed, he would hold me above the staircase as if he would drop me. I only noticed because he suddenly switched from walking while carrying me to my room to standing still for a while. I was not scared while he was doing this. He would then proceed to my bedroom and lay me down in my bed. I could not respect him as a child and never felt a strong connection between his side of the family and me, except for his mother.

Grandmother Wilhelmina or "Oma Willie," as we would call her, was a rather flamboyant lady with a high-pitched voice and overly confident to a level of slight arrogance. She was a true matriarch. My Oma Willie had nine sons, two daughters, and countless grand and great-grandchildren. Every time I visited her house, there was another child there that I had never met before. Then my oma would explain in a tone as if I was supposed to know that the child was my cousin, the son or daughter from this uncle or that aunt. My grandmother's house was always full of food and South American music. Once one entered her house, you would be offered a meal and homemade baked treats. Many of my uncles and cousins would go there just to eat. I did not like her cooking very much. My Oma always made South American dishes often based on or complemented by meat. I did not and still do not like that type of food, especially meat. My mother would always cook typical Western

European dishes which are much simpler and much more to my preference.

My Oma would absolutely not like it when I did not eat from her. She had this thing that if you visit her, you have to eat. She always made me feel at home and let me do whatever I wanted if I stayed at her house. One year I stayed with her all summer. It was one of the most enjoyable summers of my life. There was a change of company every day, whether it was cousins I was unfamiliar with, or knew personally. That summer we celebrated her birthday as well. There must have been at least 100 people coming and going that day. Besides my father, my other eight uncles are all musicians as well. They all each play a different instrument. My father played trumpet, drums, and he sang. My father and his brothers reminded me of the Jackson Five. They were very talented and musically in sync with one another.

On my grandmother's birthday that summer, they surprised her with a music performance. I believe it was the South-American version of "Happy Birthday." It was very intense, emotionally charged and soulful. Every mother would probably get emotional seeing her nine sons perform so beautifully for her, so flawlessly and with such passion. However, my Oma Willie sat in her rocking chair with her chin raised listening carefully with a slight smile on her face, rocking back and forward. Her arms fully stretched out on the arm rests while watching and listening to the performance as if she expected nothing less from her nine sons. Everybody looked up to her, was always there for her, and respected her.

Oma Willie was not so fond of my mother. My mother too is a person who carries a lot of pride and had refused to call Oma Willie "mama." My mother told her that she only had one mother who passed away and no one would replace her. Of course, this did not sit well with Oma Willie. Oma Willie was a religious Catholic lady who used to sing in the church choir. She was a soprano and always boasted about being the best in her choir. She sang for me once in her later years to show off her singing skills as I am a soprano as well. I was not impressed at all by her singing and found it to be completely out of tune, but I did not comment on it. Oma was too proud of herself.

When I was thirteen, I still played with toys. I had a big imagination and would always imagine how my life would be as an adult with dolls, Playmobil, Legos, anything that could represent people, and a household. One day while I was playing, a commercial came on television of an up-and-coming fourteen-year-old opera singer from Wales called Charlotte Church. I was not even really paying much attention to the commercial. However, when it ended, I sarcastically mimicked what she was singing. To my mother's and my own surprise, I sounded rather impressive. I was surprised at the sound of my own voice and immediately started to look into this singer. My mother purchased her album and I became obsessed with studying all the pieces on her album. They were covered songs by famous classical composers and operas. My mother was very supportive of my newfound talent and suggested that I visit the Conservatory of Amsterdam, which is the biggest music college in Holland.

My high school was not too far from the conservatory. Therefore, one afternoon after school I jumped on my bike and headed to the conservatory. It was a big old building, designed in typical Dutch style with intricate moldings. It felt somewhat intimidating. I remember thinking to myself, "Where do I start?" I walked up the big steps and went inside. There was a receptionist. "Good afternoon!" I greeted her. "I am a soprano and want to learn here." The receptionist looked at me, not sure if I was serious or not and asked me, "Learn here? What exactly would you like to learn baby? How old are you?" I responded, "Fourteen!" She slightly scoffed and told me that I was way too young. She told me that their youngest students were at least eighteen. Even though I felt rejected, almost scorned to the core, I could not just accept her sole opinion and walk away. So, I said, "Singing opera is my passion. I am really good at it. There must be some sort of program that I could do here. Where else could I go?"

After me staring at her for a brief moment, she replied, "Sweetheart, I just don't know, we don't have such young students here, I am sorry, there is nothing we can do for you." She looked at me, waiting for me to leave, but I looked back at her, hoping for some sort of a different helpful answer or alternative. "This is a college. You are too young to study here." She concluded.

I did not know how to respond to her, because by law, she was correct, I guess. I looked at her for a few more seconds as if she was wrong for trying to shoo me away, and said in a way as if I tried to intimidate her, "I really would like to speak to your supervisor."

She leaned back in her chair and looked at me surprised and hopeless at the same time. All of a sudden, she said, "Wait here." She stepped back, and moments later, she came out with another woman. This lady was in her 50s, I believe. She was a professional opera singer herself, from Germany. She was much friendlier than the receptionist. Her name was Inge.

With a heavy German accent, the lady asked me, "Hi, what's your name?"

I told her my name and explained right away why I was there.

She responded, "Well, let's hear!" and walked away, automatically assuming that I would follow her, but I was so surprised by this sudden shift of energy going from negative to positive that I froze there for a few seconds and had to adjust. She motioned to me to follow her with a smile on her face, and so I did. She took me to a beautiful room. It could have been a ballroom; it had Renaissance-style moldings, a gigantic chandelier, and windows. It was drenched in daylight and overlooked a busy street where trams passed by constantly. A few steps towards the corner of the room was a beautiful grand piano. Inge stood across from me in the middle of the room and told me to repeat what she did. I had to do some breathing exercises and ranging to prepare me for singing.

"Very good! Beautiful! Which arias do you know?" she asked me.

The question came a little unexpectedly. "Uh... I can sing 'Bist du bei mir' from Bach?" I said in a questionable tone in case she did not know the aria.

"Perfect!" she said and started playing it on the piano without sheet music while looking at me to make sure that I would start singing at the right moment.

As I sang "Bist du bei mir," she was looking at me the entire time with her mouth half open. Besides listening to my voice, she was also observing my body language, breathing, and singing technique. Once finished, she said, "You definitely have a lovely voice, absolutely lovely, but it needs a lot of polishing my dear."

I thought, "Duh! That's why I am here." But I would not have dared to insult her in any way.

She continued, "We usually never train anyone below 18 years old, but you are special and perhaps we will make an exception for you through a special private program." She looked at me in silence still thinking about my training within the conservatory.

"Thank you so much!" I said.

She showed a small polite smile with half-closed eyes in responds to my excitement and asked me to wait by the entrance for someone else to discuss application, audition, and tuition fees. I almost fell off my chair when I learned that the daily tuition was four times more than what I earned at the cheese store where I worked one day a week. Their tuition fees discouraged me but I did not show it. I was given application forms, an audition date and was sent on my way.

I gave up. There was no way that I could pay such a fee and I highly doubted that my mother would pay it.

When my mother arrived home from work, I told her about my trip to the conservatory and the tuition fees. Even though I could clearly see that there was some doubt in my mother's face, she responded, "Well...let's just go for it!" I was flabbergasted and confused. Usually when I ask my mother for an extra few euro on top of my allowance for whatever reason, she looks at me as if I am crazy. She would yell, "Excuse me? What are you asking me? Money does not grow on trees madam. You work and can use your own money." She always gave me a really hard time when I asked for a few extra euros. One time she forced me to give her all my earnings for months because I racked up the home phone bill. But now without a doubt, she agrees to pay a fortune to the conservatory? I was shocked by her response and confused, yet thinking "Whatever."

I was even more nervous on my audition date than I was when I stepped into the conservatory for the first time, blindly demanding that they train me. There was another secretary at the front desk this time. I explained to her why I was there. She looked at me with a sarcastic smile in disbelief and also asked, "How old are you?"

"Fourteen," I responded.

She continued to stare at me for a few seconds and then shook her head a little bit to wake herself up and asked me for my name. I told her. "Sara" She looked down at something on her desk that I could not see. It was probably a list. She called over to someone else's desk to let them know I was here.

"You can have a seat. They will be right with you."

I had to wait at least 30 minutes before I was led to that same room I did my first audition in. Inge was already there with another gentleman.

"Here she is! Beautiful girl with a beautiful voice!" she said.

"Ja, but she is a baby Inge," the gentleman replied.

"Sara, this is Mr. Haas. He is the intake director for the vocal department here at the conservatory," Inge said.

"I have heard a lot about you, Sara," the man added. He too was clearly German and a bit old-fashioned.

I felt very intimidated by Mr. Haas. I had a strong feeling that he knew the opera field, every composer, every aria, and everything else about it like the back of his hand. He practically looked like Mozart himself!

Inge asked me if I had warmed up, which made me even more nervous because I had not. Inge looked at me surprised and asked, "Then what were you doing in the past half an hour?"

"I was waiting in the lobby. The lady behind the counter told me to sit and wait, so I did," I responded.

Mr. Haas rubbed his forehead with his index finger and thumb. Inge angrily told him in German that they really must stop putting random volunteers at the front desk. I was thinking to myself that maybe this "random volunteer" just did not take me seriously.

While Mr. Haas looked over my paperwork, he asked, "You are fourteen. Did your mother sign off on this?"

"Yes, she did," I replied.

"Where are your parents?" he asked.

"My parents are working," I replied.

"How long have you been singing? There is not much of a background here."

"One year," I replied.

He looked up at me from my application wondering if I was joking.

Inge responded quickly in German, assuming that I would not understand her while I was learning German heavily in school and was in Germany on a regular basis, "Es gibt niemanden wie sie, ich verspreche das sie etwas besondered ist."

I will never forget those words. I even remember the calming and melodious tone in her voice while she was saying this. It means "There is nobody like her, I promise that she is exceptional."

I was there thinking in my fourteen-year-old head, "Why am I exceptional? There are so many other sopranos who are so much more advanced than I am." I wondered if it had to do with the fact that not many people of color sing opera, or the fact that I was fourteen years old.

Inge did a quick warm-up with me before I started to sing "Mein Herr Marquis" from Die Fledermaus. Unlike the last time, now she looked at me with pride as I sang while she accompanied me on the piano. Once finished, there was no expression on the face of Mr. Haas at all. I could not figure out if he liked it or not. After a few seconds of complete silence Mr. Haas asked me if I could do a piece with Lento to Largo speed? I almost fainted. I thought, "What in this world does Lento and Largo mean? Does it even genuinely mean anything at all?"

Inge could read my face. She said, "Mr. Haas wants to know if you can sing a piece of lower speed so we can see your breathing techniques better and observe how you control them. Which aria do you know that has a slower pace?"

"Barcarole...from Offenbach?" I replied.

Mr. Haas looked at me annoyed and responded, "That is a duet Sara. We would need two Saras for that. We only have one."

Inge asked, "Do you know Plaisir D'Amour?"

Mr. Haas said, "Ah, the easiest aria, of course."

"Yes, I do know that aria," I responded, completely ignoring Mr. Haas's negative remark. "I can sing that."

Once finished it was again difficult to read Mr. Haas's face. He and Inge were whispering in German before Inge said, "Thank you sweetheart. We will process your application, and I will call you this week, ja?"

I left feeling completely discouraged. I had a sour feeling about their final decision but decided not to stress about it. I rode home on my bicycle telling myself to forget about the conservatory. The sun set early that evening and I carried on with my usual activities. About a week later, I received a phone call from Inge.

"Hi Sara, how are you? How do you feel?" she asked me.

"What have you decided?" I asked impatiently ignoring her question.

"Well, we love you. You are special, and we want to train you!"

I could not believe my ears. Three days a week, after regular high school, I attended the conservatory. I took it very seriously and improved rapidly. Even though I was so much younger than the rest, I certainly was not treated any differently. It was a serious, no-nonsense atmosphere. I was proud of being trained at the great Conservatory of Amsterdam. To me, it validated my talent. I believed in myself even more. While I was attending the Conservatory of Amsterdam, I performed a lot around the Netherlands, usually in smaller theaters and as an opening act for much larger events. My performances were always greatly admired and respected by young and old. It was not common to hear a teenager of color sing opera. It was always my dream to combine opera with modern music.

16-year-old me during an opera performance.

Alisa

Besides performing all over the Netherlands, I was babysitting for different families to earn an extra income as well. On December 31, 2002, I received a phone call from a parent I babysat for on a regular basis. A neighbor of her wanted to go to a party that evening and asked me if I could babysit her two daughters. One of her daughters was four years old and the other was just a few months old. With my mother's approval, the children were brought to our house to spend the night.

The moment the mother and her two daughters entered our house, I immediately felt that those kids would be part of my life for a long time. The oldest four-year-old girl's name was Cindy. She was an adorable blonde, brisk little girl in cowboy boots and a tiger-print faux-fur jacket. She spoke as if she had the world all figured out. It was clear that this was not the first time she had stayed over at a stranger's house as she felt just way too comfortable. Her little sister Alisa was a sweet innocent baby with the cutest round face framed in a lot of chestnut-colored hair that swirled in all directions on her round head. Alisa's father happened to be my mother's cousin's son, so she had a different father than her older sister Cindy.

My mother and I felt like something was wrong with Alisa. When she arrived, she was sleeping. Upon dropping her off, her mother was very careful and cautioned us to be quiet and not wake her up without explaining why. When she did wake up, she was just crying hysterically with her eyes shut. She was not screaming in a way like, "Where is my mother and where am I?" It was just hysterically screeching as if she was in severe agony. I felt so terrible and an instant sense of responsibility towards her in particular.

The next day, their mother called and asked if the girls could stay one more night. She did not explain why but I was more than happy to keep them longer. The following day when their mother picked them up, I told her that she could always reach out to me if she needed help. That same week, she called me and asked if I could take Alisa for a few nights, as Cindy would be with her biological father.

It was snowing that morning when I left to pick her up. Alisa was brought downstairs in her stroller and handed over to me like a big bag of potatoes or something. I was pushing the stroller in a daze thinking "really? Did this really happen just now?" While looking at this innocent sleeping baby. She looked dirty, greasy and carried a stale smell of a mixture of baby wipes, not being washed and cigarette smoke. I looked into the diaper bag where all her necessities were kept. The bag was filthy, and just as expected, it was stuffed with dirty unfolded clothing. These clothes all had lost their original colors from being washed incorrectly. There were no socks in the bag. The only things I could actually use were diapers and formula milk. I felt like I had a responsibility to take care of her.

Instead of heading home, I headed to a thrift store to pick up some decent second-hand baby clothing for her. I was just a teenager myself, a student, and my income was meager. I did not have the funds to buy brand-new clothing for her. In addition, I purchased some baby care products. I washed the second-hand clothes and gave her a thorough bath. Then I put her in a diaper while her newly purchased clothes were in the dryer. She was clean, fed and slept for hours straight. Even though I felt so heartbroken for Alisa, I really enjoyed this new responsibility of "having a baby." She would spend most of the time at my house moving forward.

I slowly purchased more and more second-hand baby items. I bought a crib, a better, cleaner and cozier stroller, a bike seat, and a burgundy faux-fur winter jacket with matching hat. Everything a baby needed, I made sure that I had it for her. I would purchase all of her organic food at a local whole-food store. I would bring her to day-care if I had to go to school, and to the doctor if she was not feeling well. Sometimes when I brought her back to her parents, I had to give them updates on what sort of foods she eats now and updates from the doctor. It was sad really, but I was happy to be able to be there for this little girl. She called me "mama" too and truly believed that I was her mother. I don't even think her mother ever minded.

Alisa was two years old when I left for New York. She continued visiting my mother on a regular basis and came to New York several times to visit me shortly after I moved away.

Alisa 8 months old.

Alisa five-years old

Alisa today.

March 3, 2004

It was March 3, 2004, and I had just turned 18. Wow! I am 18 years old! I felt no different than the previous day, except for the fact that I am now allowed to make all my own decisions. I no longer needed permission from my mother! I prepared myself mentally to move to New York. However, I had not been able to buy a flight ticket yet because I was underage and my mother wouldn't purchase a ticket for me, not even with my own money on my behalf. I went to a local travel agency known for providing affordable flight tickets. They were big on selling flights to far away destinations that had many stopovers. If your final destination was one of those stopovers, it was very likely that you could score a very affordable flight. I got a flight to Singapore with a stopover in New York City.

I booked a one-way flight and packed all my belongings into two suitcases. I was more than ready to leave the Netherlands, which I found to be so mundane, slow and boring. On the day I left, my mother was weeping at the airport. She wept so loudly that one would think that I would never return to the Netherlands again. Now I think about what I would do, how I would handle my 18-year-old daughter moving to the city. Now that I realize how much could have gone wrong, I am not sure if I would let my daughter go by herself. I was super naive yet stubborn as could be. On top of that, my English was very basic at the time.

I arrived on a warm, sunny day in March. As soon as I stepped out of the airplane, I could immediately sense the bustling energy. You could already hear it in the voices of the airport workers. They spoke fast and energetically as if every sentence was supposed to be followed by "Come on! Keep it moving!" while they were waiting for each other's answers. Once I got to customs, I felt like I was being interrogated for committing crime. I came from the Netherlands which is a soft, cushy and comfortable place compared to New York.

"Why are you here ma'am? How are you going to support yourself? Where will you live? What brought you here? Did you bring any food?"

I looked at the customs agent as if he was speaking Chinese because he spoke so fast, and responded with "Hah?"

The customs agent looked at me annoyed. He clearly did not have much patience. He pointed at the word "food" on the declaration card and said, "Food ma'am, f-o-o-d food did you bring any food?"

I was there thinking, "Is it illegal to bring food to New York or something? Why is he so paranoid about food?" Then I answered, "No food." I felt a bit guilty not telling him that I had the pretzels they gave me on the airplane in my hand luggage. It felt like he would throw me in prison if I had told him. I grabbed my luggage and decided to take one of those yellow taxis you see in those American movies.

"Where are you going?" the driver asked with a heavy Asian accent.

I had no idea where I was going. I just wanted to be in New York City. He waited for my answer. "Where can I go? I don't know. I just want to be in New York City," I thought. "Where can I go in New York? Times Square. Please go there," I said in my broken English with a heavy stubby Dutch accent. He pulls out and headed to Times Square. I was amazed that he understood me and knew exactly where Times Square was. I was contemplating what "going to Times Square" meant to me at that moment, and what it meant to the taxi driver. For me, it was an exciting and incredible experience to be so close to Times Square. Something I have lived for and looked forward to for years. However, for the taxi driver, it was most probably just another stop to drop off passengers and an annoying and busy place where traffic is usually so incredibly dense.

The taxi driver dropped me and my two suitcases off in the middle of Times Square. Literally in the middle of that Island-like part of Times Square. I stood there absolutely in awe of the scene. I felt like I was on top of the world. At the same time, I was wondering, "How did I get here? What in the world am I doing here?" There was noise everywhere, from car horns to music to commercials, to people talking in a thousand different languages. The experience was so enriching. Nobody looked funny at me because everybody was funny, different and interesting themselves. I stood there for at least half an hour before it even crossed my mind that I should start thinking about where to go next. I could not move away from the spot the taxi driver dropped me because my suitcases were too big and too heavy for me to move both at once.

I needed to take another taxi. Yellow cabs were racing all around me. I needed to find a pay-phone to call the yellow cab company and ask them to pick me up. I was wondering what their phone number is. I left my suitcases on the spot and walked into a Starbucks across the street to ask if they knew the phone number of the yellow cab company. I watched my suitcases like an eagle while standing in line at Starbucks.

"Hallo,... uhm, uhm... do you maybe know the phone number for the yellow cabs?" I asked.

A young lady looked at me puzzled and replied, "Phone number for them yellow cabs? What do you mean by phone number?"

I explained to her that I was trying to get a cab to take me to a hotel.

"Girl, where are you from? You just hold them; you don't call them, you can't call them."

I was absolutely dumbfounded. After a few seconds, she explained what she meant with "holding them" by extending her arm and waving her hand. "That's all you got to do when you see one of them coming your way, okay baby? One will stop for you."

"What?" I couldn't believe that this was their normal accepted system of getting a cab. I was thinking, "What a chutzpah to just demand a taxi to pull over like that in the first place. And how silly it must look to even stand there with your arm extended like that. What if the taxi doesn't stop and hits my arm?" I felt stressed already. I stood by my luggage and watched the taxis drive by. I was observing them first. They seemed to drive a lot faster than all the other cars. "Perhaps there is a certain spot where they stop often or drive slower. I would be much more comfortable extending my arm at such a spot," I thought.

Luckily for me, a passenger got out of a yellow cab near where I was. I ran almost frantically to the taxi and asked the driver if he could take me to a hotel. He motioned for me to get in. I pointed to my luggage, and he stepped out of the car to help me load them in.

"Where are you going?" he asked but this time with an African accent.

I didn't know what to tell him because I didn't know where I was going. "What are some other places here?" I was thinking. "Ah!... Wall Street with the Dow Jones and stuff. I hear that on the news in the Netherlands all the time." I was thinking

"That hotel on Wall Street, do you know?" I asked.

The cab driver was a little amused by this answer and joyfully said, "There are so many hotels on Wall Street. This is New York! Do I look like I have a glass ball or something, and know which hotel you want to go to? Do you even know where you are going to? Which of the hotels would you like to go?"

I did not want to sound too stupid, so I answered, "Oh I forgot the name. Could you please name a few?"

He started to mention some hotels. They all sounded so expensive until he said, "Club Quarters?" The word "quarters" made this hotel sound affordable to me. I only had $360, left so the cheaper the better.

"Yes! That's the one! Please take me there."

I arrived near Wall Street in the financial district of Manhattan. "Ugh, so dead here!" I was thinking. The area felt gloomy and boring. I wondered, "Where are all those aggressive Wall Street business people like you see on the news and in the movies?" This is nothing like Times Square. I was in front of a high building that had "Club Quarters" written in golden letters. This does not look like an affordable hotel at all, but I felt like I had no choice at that point. I walked in and booked one night for $140, and after that, I walked right back outside to look for something to eat. In the hotel lobby, I asked the lady behind the counter where I could buy food. She started to give me a million and one options, ending with "or you can just go to the deli across the street." I was confused. "To the Deli? What in the world is she talking about? What is a deli? Isn't that the capital city of India?" I wondered. She could read my confusion but did not realize what exactly was going through my head. "Right over there, about a block away," she said in a friendly tone. "They have good stuff too." She pointed in the direction I should go.

I found the place, which seemed like a luncheonette to me. They were selling all sorts of stuff; however, I was used to eating a simple slice of multi-grain bread with Gouda cheese on it. The deli did not have this. Instead, I saw whole cheeses in the shape of bricks and loose breads. "How much is a piece of bread with a slice of cheese?" I asked.

"Five dollars," he replied.

"Five dollars?!" I asked, surprised as if he was crazy.

He looked at me surprised. He collected himself quickly and started to show me the different cheeses. In the Netherlands, a loaf of bread and a pack of eight slices of cheese cost less than five dollars. "Maybe he is the type of person that everybody at home was warning me about? "Maybe he wants to rip me off," I thought. He tried to start a friendly conversation by asking where I was from and so on. I was so insulted by him trying to "rip me off" by trying to charge five bucks for one sandwich with one slice of cheese on it, that I left the deli and bought a cupcake for one dollar and fifty cents at one of those street stands instead.

I bought a prepaid cell phone for over 100 dollars, and I was almost completely broke. Even though I was scared and didn't know what to do, I was excited at the same time. I kind of loved the challenge of having to figure out what to do. I remember calling my best friend on my new cell phone and explaining my situation to her. She was more worried than I was and urged me to call my mother and to go back to the Netherlands, but I refused. I told her not to alarm my mother and hung up.

I decided to rest for the day. I was tired. "I will figure out what to do in the morning," I told myself. I fell asleep with the television on and the windows of my hotel room open. I was woken up by the sound of heels walking down the street. "Click clack click clack". It was the voices of typical American broadcasters on television. I looked out of the window and saw those business people I was looking for the previous day passing by on their way to work. I started to get excited all over again. I was in New York! Yes! But I almost ran out of money and hadn't figured out what to do to support myself. "I can pay for this hotel for one more night, but I would be completely broke if I booked another night," I thought. "Perhaps I have to start by finding a more affordable hotel or a short-term room for rent or something. I should start looking for a job as well."

I asked the receptionist at the hotel where there was an internet café. She explained that the hotel offers computers with internet access for guests to use for free. I found a much more affordable place to stay at called the YMCA on the Upper Westside of Manhattan. It was about forty dollars a night for a single private room with a shared bathroom. "Yuck! A shared bathroom?" I cringed at the thought of having to share a bathroom with other people. I took a yellow cab to the YMCA hotel. The cab drove through a scenic green area right after driving through high-rise areas. I wondered where I was. "I don't think you have to leave Manhattan to get to the hotel. Is this guy trying to kidnap me or something?" I was thinking.

"Where are we?" I asked the cab driver.

"This is Central Park!" he replied. "Is this your first time here?" he asked.

I didn't want to answer his question. I thought, "What if I tell him and he tries to rip me off like the guy from the deli?"

"No," I responded in a rather uninviting tone.

The YMCA hotel certainly did not look as lavish as Club Quarters did. The room was quite simple and I had to take my suitcases to my room by myself. The room had a twin bed with a folded blanket and towel on it. It also had a small desk with a chair and a television hanging in the top corner. It reminded me of the look of those American jail cell rooms you see in movies. However, I was grateful to have a place to sleep and happy to be safe.

I left my room to find a pair of bath slippers. There was no way I would step into those showers with my bare feet. I would tie plastic bags to my ankles if I had to. I asked one of the hotel's cleaning staff if the hotel had any complimentary slippers. He must have been a college student or something. He looked at me as if I was crazy. I thought, "Of course, how can I expect this place to have complimentary slippers? I would probably be lucky if they had a small tube of complimentary toothpaste."

"I want free slippers for the douche," I said. "Douche" means "shower" in Dutch. I didn't realize it meant something different in America.

"No, we don't have slippers for whatever you need them for," he replied. "But anyway, there is a pharmacy. It's just a few blocks down Central Park West. They probably sell them."

"What is a pharmacy?" I asked. "Is that a store?"

"Where are you from?" he asked curiously while taking a more comfortable posture.

"Europa," I answered impatiently. "What is the name of this place I can buy slippers?"

"Just a regular drug store," he replied. "I don't remember the name. Have a great day." He walked away. He was clearly insulted.

I kept wondering what he meant by drug store. "Are drugs legal here? Or this guy is just trying to mess with me." I decided to just look around for a store that sells bathroom slippers. I was already tired of these Americans constantly asking me, "Where are you from? Where are you from?" and then trying to pull a trick on me.

Eventually I found a pharmacy called Duane Reade right at the location the young fellow at the hotel told me. Besides selling painkillers and other medications, they sell cookies, candies, cheese, sodas and all sorts of random non-pharmaceutical stuff. I even saw toys in one of their aisles! In the Netherlands, pharmacies sell pharmaceutical products only. After taking a look at the drugs, I realized that the word "drugs" has a much broader definition in America. They had beautiful bathroom slippers right at the entrance. I just wanted a pair of simple cheap rubber bath slippers but they didn't have exactly that. I bought a pair with big puffy pink dahlia-like flowers on top of them, along with some snacks. I ripped the glued-on flowers off when I got back to the hotel.

In great discomfort I took a shower and watched television as I wondered what to do next. I fell asleep early again and woke up late in the evening. I knew that I would not be able to fall asleep anytime soon, so I decided to go out to find an internet café. I walked to a large internet café on 42nd street right by Times Square. Manhattan was alive! The streets were busy and all the stores were still open! I was completely thrilled. You can hardly get a carton of milk after 6 p.m. in Holland, let alone a full-blown shopping adventure! I stood there, taking in all the energy that the city was radiating. Everything was just so beautiful and new to me.

I noticed how life was made so convenient for New Yorkers too. Whatever you needed would be no further than a few blocks away. You could walk, take a bus, a cab, the train and even a rickshaw! I guess it depends on what mood one is in when deciding which means of transportation you would take. Everything from random paraphernalia to clothing to elaborate cakes was just accessible everywhere. "Cakes for what?" I was thinking. To me, this was just a crazy fantasy world. Where I am from, for such cakes, you place an order way in advance at one of the few bakeries who are specialized in making such cakes, and you have to travel to pick them up. In Manhattan, you can just cross a street at midnight and get such an elaborate cake from Wholefoods. I purchased a small pre-folded laminated map of Manhattan at a stand selling candies and all sorts of tourist items and just walked everywhere at the beginning using this map as a bible.

As I sat at the computer at the internet cafe, I felt like I was being a bit unrealistic expecting to find some sort of work in one day. I thought, "Who is going to hire me the next day? Perhaps I should look for a short-term rental instead of staying in hotels." I first checked to see if I had any new emails. I received one email from someone I didn't know with the subject line "Nederlandse au-pair" which means "Dutch au-pair." I opened the email and read it. It was an email from a Dutch family living in Westchester New York. They were looking for a Dutch au-pair to live with them and help them out with their three children three days a week. The remaining four days are your free days, and you can do whatever you want. I wondered, "How did they get my email address?" I used to babysit a lot in the Netherlands. They probably got my information from one of the parents of the children I used to watch. I got excited and sent a message back with my phone number.

On my way back to the YMCA, I was thinking, "Westchester? Where in the world is that? How far from Manhattan could that be?" I received a phone call from the mother of that family that same evening. She was so excited to find a Dutch au-pair here in New York to care for her children. It was very important to her that her children continue to speak Dutch at home. That following morning, the whole family picked me and my two suitcases up from the YMCA in their minivan.

18-year-old me

Au-Pair for Family Scheutema

There was a lot of excitement in the minivan. The mother, Leontien was sitting next to the father, Jean-Luuk, who was driving, and I was sitting in the first row of the back seat next to baby Jasper. Behind us sat nine-year-old Floris and eight-year-old Samantha. Jean-Luuk was a calm and intelligent man. He did not say much but you could tell that he was always alert and thinking. Jean-Luuk was a short, stocky man with a broad face and with a very slight smirk on his face most of the time. He was always very kind, confident and had a very sarcastic sense of humor, sometimes a little annoying. He was the biological father of baby Jasper only. Floris and Samantha had a different biological father from their mother's previous marriage. Their mother, a mouthy red-head who "knew everything" and absolutely loved to be in full control of absolutely everything at all times, even of your truth. If she had her mind set on her version of the truth, no one could convince her otherwise. On the other hand, she always made sure that everybody was happy and had what they needed, including me.

Then we have Floris, a handsome boy with jet-black hair and sky-blue eyes. The contrast between his hair and eyes was striking. He was a wise boy. In the car, he was the one who elatedly explained everybody's business and the daily routines and stuff. His mother let Floris do all the talking, corrected and added to his explanations here and there while proudly letting him speak. Samantha was a dark-blonde sweet girl who loved to laugh and have fun but was extremely stubborn. The stubbornness she had inherited from her mother, and it was her mother who knew best how to deal with her in a conflict. Her stepfather did not know how to deal with it well, but he loved his stepdaughter very much. Samantha instantly embraced me as her big sister. They were very caring. If there was any type of shower gel or breakfast cereal that I wanted, then I would not have to pay for it. Their mother would get it just as she would for her other children. It was a pleasant ride on a sunny day. It felt good. I felt that they were happy with me and excited to learn more about me.

The Scheutemas lived in a beautiful large house on a small hill in Westchester. This was a temporary rental house they lived in while Jean-Luuk was stationed in New York. I had my own bed and bathroom on the third floor of the house. It was a cozy room that looked out over the backyard. They gave me clean linen and a radio for if I wanted to listen to music or something. I was very happy with the radio. I found this radio station that played music from the sixties which gave me a soothing nostalgic feeling. My mother would often play golden oldies when I was a young child, and besides that, I am really fond of golden oldies. As I was listening to all this music, I would experience all sorts of warm and colorful sensations. I cannot exactly describe it. Ever since I can remember, I was always a spiritual type of child who would have thoughts and experiences more so in feelings instead of words. Words could not even describe it. It is similar to listening to classical music. As you listen, you may feel or see a whole story that corresponds with the music even though you only hear instruments and no words are used.

Approximately an hour after we arrived at the house, mother Leontien suggested that we should all go to the grocery store to get food that I like to eat.

"I eat yoghurt with cruesli for breakfast," I told her while we were roaming the isles.

"Well, we don't have cruesli here in America!" she said in a way to make her family laugh. She showed me some other products which supposedly are similar to Dutch yoghurt and cruesli. cruesli is very similar to granola.

The following morning, I tried American yoghurt with cruesli. Wow, that tasted so mighty compared to Dutch yoghurt. The American yoghurt has the heavy consistency of Dutch cottage cheese or something, and the granola obviously has twenty times more sugar than the Dutch cruesli. The first time that mother Leontien started to cook dinner, I explained to her that I am vegetarian. Aside from this, I cannot eat meat and milk products together.

"Huh...why not?" she asked.

"Because I am Jewish, and one of our basic rules of keeping kosher is not to mix meat and milk products together," I replied.

Mother Leontien rolled her eyes and responded, "Well, I don't have two sinks and I am not getting two sinks for you either," she said.

I felt so insulted. "Well, I never asked for two sinks, Leontien," I responded and walked away.

The two older children Floris and Samantha taught me a lot of English. They had been to a regular American school for years before so their English was much better than mine. I would often commute to Manhattan on the train on the weekends. I really wanted to be there rather than in Westchester. After three months living with the Scheutemas in Westchester, I told myself, "You did not come to New York to live in boring Westchester taking care of other people's kids." So, I made up my mind to leave this family and move to Manhattan.

I decided to look for another family who lives in Manhattan and needs a babysitter. I posted an ad on a website that matches families with babysitters and quickly found yet another family with an Asian mother and Dutch father. They too wanted a babysitter to speak Dutch to their baby. Mother Leontien was not happy about this. She felt that I should have informed her of what my plans were, way before I made the decision to leave them. Today, I think she was absolutely right, but back then, I did not know what kind of reaction to expect from her. I didn't think it was safe to tell her. I was worried, "what if she throws me right out on the street?" I knew she liked to be in control. She was not in control of my decision, so I was simply not comfortable telling her right away. I didn't know how big of a tantrum she would throw and on what level.

Family Jansen

I was so happy to be back in Manhattan. Sleeping and waking up in bustling Manhattan. I found a furnished room for rent in West Harlem on 123rd Street. It was not my plan to rent a room in Harlem. As in the Bronx, Harlem had an infamous reputation in the Netherlands. The Dutch say, "You stay away from Harlem because there are a lot of drug dealers, prostitutes, and junkies that will rob you and hurt you there." We thought that Harlem still was the same as it was back in the eighties. My budget was super low and a room in Harlem was all I could afford. I went to see the room, and took the 2 train from Times Square to 125th Street.

It was a beautiful summer day. I remember so vividly the amazing, different, urban energy hanging in Harlem as I climbed up the stairs at the train station on 125th Street at Malcolm X Boulevard. The busy 125th Street was packed with African Americans, Hispanics and sprinkled with a few Caucasian people. All these different ethnic groups were relaxed and comfortable walking the streets. Nobody seemed to be nervous about drug dealers, junkies and prostitutes. Children with all sorts of artistic braids and beads in their hair were playing jump-rope in front of brownstone buildings. This was exactly how I saw Harlem on television in the Netherlands, and how I envisioned it to be. I did not feel unsafe at all, on the contrary. I felt very safe in that environment.

Harlem has its own authentic vibe like no other. As I strolled the streets, I noticed different smells in the air as I passed those street stands selling perfumes, oils, shea butter and essences. I could smell the fried chicken as I passed Popeyes. People seemed a bit more relaxed here than in Manhattan. They seemed happier as well. Friendlier, enjoying life more.

I found my new address on 123rd Street at St. Nicholas Avenue. I rang the bell and a friendly short, heavy-set Hispanic lady opened the door. Her name was Carmen and she had about five dogs.

"I am here to look at the room," I said in an uncertain tone.

She grabbed the keys and led me up the steps of the brownstone building, and then one flight up the stairs inside the building. All the way down the hallway at the very end was a cute, modestly furnished room. It was just big enough to hold a twin bed and a small desk. The room had a built-in wardrobe and there was a simple spacious bathroom at the other end of the floor which I had to share with two other roommates. Next to my room, there lived an older gentleman. His name was Manny and he was Carmen's older brother. Manny did not have any teeth. He was skinny and about my height. He was a true gentleman; he was always willing to help and was very respectful of my privacy. He took care of the maintenance in the building in exchange for a free room. I took the room and moved in right away.

I went to meet the Jansen family who had a 6-month-old baby, Bridgitte. Mr. Jansen was Dutch. He was a very tall blonde man with a weak mind. He was very gullible, highly susceptible to his wife's dominance, and a true pushover, which was something I wasn't used to with Dutch men. Mrs. Jansen was a short Chinese lady who was super skinny. Her body reminded me of that of a fourteen-year-old boy as there was no actual feminine figure. She had a large head, and with her short puffy hairdo, her head even seemed much larger than it really was. Mr. and Mrs. Jansen were both immigration lawyers. They met in law school.

Mrs. Jansen was clearly the dominant one in that marriage. She desperately wanted to be associated with Dutch culture. She was not happy if her husband spoke Dutch to me, and she was unable to join the conversation. One time, her husband shared how people often think that he adopted Bridgette when he is outside with her alone. Mrs. Jansen was certainly not happy that he shared that. Bridgitte indeed looked much more Asian than she did Caucasian. They lived in a small odd triangle shaped corner studio apartment near City Hall in downtown Manhattan. The apartment was on the 26th floor. Bridgitte was a sweet little girl with a round face and loads of jet-black thick straight hair. She had so much hair for such a little baby that you could almost believe it was a wig. She would never fuzz without a good reason and it was a breeze and pleasure to take care of her.

One day, Bridgitte's maternal grandmother came to visit from China. We could not get along at all from the beginning. Her grandmother had a very hard time speaking English and she was always shaking a little bit. Bridgitte's grandmother constantly wanted to boss me around, and of course, I was not happy with that. So, I ignored her demands throughout her stay. She probably felt powerless because of her shaking body and inability to communicate and understand what is being said around her in English, so she may have been trying to have some kind of control over me and her granddaughter to make herself feel better, especially since she was constantly trying to judge and "correct" anything to the point of being ridiculous. It even became so silly that she told me one day to take my hand off Bridgette's stomach while Bridgette was sleeping in my lap. She was afraid that my hand was too heavy and Bridgette would not be able to breathe. I completely disobeyed and told her in so many words how ridiculous she was. Of course, she complained to her daughter about this the minute her daughter got home. Mrs. Jansen told me to listen to her mother no matter how ridiculous it may sound. Mr. Jansen however stood up for me for once as he was also frustrated himself with being bossed around by his mother-in-law. This made the situation a lot worse of course. Today, Mr. and Mrs. Jansen are divorced.

Around the same time that Mrs. Jansen's mother came to visit, I was strolling around a lot in Battery Park just thinking about everything. I thought, "I am new in New York, so I should start connecting with other Jewish people here and try to do some volunteer work or something. Where in the world do I begin here?" One morning, I was sitting on the train on my way to Bridgitte's house to babysit her. Across from me sat a young gentleman, seemingly on his way to work, reading something. This guy was wearing a *yarmulke*, which is a round head cover that religious Jewish men wear. I must have stared at him the whole time. However, he was so absorbed in whatever he was reading that thankfully he did not notice me staring at him. I decided to ask him for some guidance with regards to learning more, doing outreach work and practicing Judaism more. I was too shy to ask anybody anything on a train in front of everyone, so I waited until he got off the train. He passed the stop where I had to get off, so I stayed on the train as well.

On the last stop in Manhattan at Wall Street, he finally got up and left the train. I followed him and stood behind him on the escalator. He was no longer absorbed in his book and just looked ahead of himself while patiently waiting to reach the top. I carefully tucked the sleeve of his jacket. He looked back at me bewildered as if I was a robber who was about to rob him or something. He did not say anything and just stared at me, first bewildered, and then with a "what do you want?" look on his face, I said, "Hallo!"

"I am new in New York. I am Jewish and would like to learn more and connect with others. Would you know where I could go?" I said with my very heavy Dutch accent.

His face softened instantly. "Where are you from?" he asked.

"The Netherlands," I replied.

"How old are you? Did you convert? Is your mother Jewish? What about her mother? Are you here alone? Where are your parents? Why did you come to New York? Give me your number, and I will look into this for you."

I gave him my number, not expecting to hear back from him. That morning I quit my job with the Jansen family. I decided to take a walk again in Battery Park and sat on a bench looking over the Hudson River. The money I earned watching Bridgette was just enough for me to survive. I had no savings, but I was not worried about how I was going to pay the next month's rent for my room. The fact that I was no longer involved with Mrs. Jansen and her mother made me very happy. I was happy to have found the strength to quit instead of being fearful of losing my income if I quit or if they would let me go. Even then it was already important to me not to be stressed. My mental health and happiness were not to be jeopardized by these people. I sat and was in a meditative state, not thinking about anything or anyone. Instead, I was just listening to the waters of the Hudson River and the chatter of tourists in the background. I felt amazing and then abruptly got disturbed by the loud and obnoxious sound of my ringing cell phone. I thought that it was Bridgette's mother begging me to come back. However, she would not have the balls to call me herself. Instead, she probably told her husband to call me to convince me to come back. She knew that I liked him more than her, so she would tell him to call me. Of course, he would do so like a puppet.

I looked at my phone and I did not see the phone numbers of one of Bridgette's parents but it was a call from a strange number. "Hallo!?" I answered. It was some Rabbi. He said my phone number was passed on to him by the gentleman I approached at the Wall Street train station. I was surprised because I didn't expect to hear anything. This Rabbi had a lot of questions, trying his best to exactly figure out my Jewish roots. He clearly was made aware of that I was a person of color. After all his typical and sometimes tricky questions were answered, he suggested that I visit a non-profit organization on the Upper West Side of Manhattan that offers cultural, spiritual, educational and social events to young Jewish professionals in their 20's and 30's. It sounded exactly like what I was looking for. First, I checked out their website and then attended their class one evening. It was a warm place and very welcoming but different from what I expected. I am used to Jewish people being quiet, serious, stiff, and overall more Orthodox. However, this place felt like everybody was a hippie or something. I found the place to be modern, not so quiet, and full of futuristic mindsets. They were open and accepting of all sorts of ways of life, with creative perspectives on the Torah and so on.

The Rabbi's name was Michael Weiss. He was this young blonde gentleman with glasses. I believe he was in his forties. He seemed super cool like the cool and smart guy in college that many students would look up to and refer to for guidance. He had another Rabbi working for him as well who I found to be a perfect role model for the young community they served. His name was Alon Kaplan and he was even cooler. Rabbi Kaplan was very handsome. He was tall with dark hair, tanned skin, striking blue eyes, and a short dark beard. He always knew what to say and when and how to say it. He made sure that he knew everybody's name and gave everyone a little bit of his personal attention. Whenever he looked at you, there would always be a very slight, flirtatious smile on his face and his eyes would penetrate right through you. Especially if you needed something from him and you asked him for something, he would often allow an awkward moment of silence, while staring you down before he would answer. Rabbi Kaplan had that swag, that magic to pull people in. Everybody liked him.

The first time I visited this organization I was wearing a black long sleeve fitted top with a long Scottish skirt that had a plaid design, heavy pleads, and three small leather belts on the side. I arrived a little late but Rabbi Weiss immediately interrupted his own class and warmly welcomed me. He motioned with his arm to come in and pointed at an empty seat around the large table where everyone was sitting.

Then he introduced me to everyone as if no one heard me when I told him my name a second ago. He continued his class and I kept on getting distracted by a gentleman who kept on tapping the floor with his hideous cowboy boots. He would stop tapping and smile at me whenever I glanced at him with an annoyed look. As soon as I looked away, he would start tapping again seconds later. Of course, today I would have understood right away that he did that to catch my attention. Today I would have completely ignored it, but back then I was a lot naiver. Even though I had come to this class to learn, I was heavily observing the place and everybody around me.

The class took place in a large room on the tenth floor of an old but beautiful building that stood on a busy street on the Upper West Side of Manhattan. There was nothing but a huge table we were all sitting around and bookcases with books. There were all sorts of religious books wrapped in fancy dark colored leather bound, with embossed gold or silver writing. I had no idea what they were all about. I thought that we only had the Torah and a siddur. I was curious about all the other books that looked alike. I thought, "Why is there so much to say? Could it be that different big Rabbis want to prove their points of view about Judaism by writing books?" I could not understand.

None of the other students at the table looked anything like me. Some had heavy Israeli accents and it was clear that most of the students knew Rabbi Weiss well. Besides serious Torah learning, there was a fair amount of joking and laughing as well. The atmosphere was refreshing, except for the annoying guy with those cowboy boots. I could see why this place was recommended, how I could learn the basics, and grow in a direction that fits me without being judged.

After the class, the questions started to pour in.

"Welcome! It's so nice that you came! Where are you from? How long are you here? No way, you are here in New York alone? No way!"

I had not yet met young people like myself in New York and I enjoyed talking to them, except for the guy in the cowboy boots. He just irked me to the core for some reason. Everywhere I was standing and talking to people, he was only a few feet away staring me down with the same stupid smirk he had at the table. Eventually, he found the courage to approach me as well and spoke with an authentic New York accent.

"So nice to meet you. Will you come again on Wednesday?" he asked.

"Don't know yet" I responded.

"Well, it's nice meeting you. Have a good night." He walked away.

I went to the bathroom and started to have a conversation with two other young Israeli women who were close friends, Maya and Orli. They had been attending this class for years and were so kind. We walked out of the bathroom together, and to my surprise, the guy in the cowboy boots was waiting outside the bathroom door. Even though you could probably tell that I was a little surprised to see him standing there, I tried to keep a straight face. I ignored him as I, Maya and Orli passed by. We were waiting for the elevator to come while talking.

Soon I noticed he was also waiting for the elevator now, so I greeted Maya and Orli, and decided to take the stairs. Now he was following me down the stairs, and that was when he began to really creep me out. I started walking fast towards the train station.

"Why are you running?" he asked. "Did you have dinner already?"

I got so nervous that I could not get my English right. I wanted to ask him why he was following me. A mixture of Dutch and English came out. I said, "Stop! Stop it! Go! I already ate. Now go!"

"Let me give you a ride! My car is right here!" he said.

I did not even look back and just headed home.

Yitzchak

I avoided going to Rabbi Weiss his classes for a week or two, and the next time I went, that dude with the cowboy boots wasn't there. I continued to attend the classes and made new friends until one evening, the cowboy boots guy was there again! He wasn't wearing those hideous boots this time. He apologized for chasing me the last time. He was very careful about initiating a conversation this time, but when he did, he actually seemed much more pleasant than last time. His name was Yitzchak and he lived in Westchester NY. He had a New York accent with a slight Spanish hint to it. He had a glass company in Yonkers, and all his employees were Mexican and Puerto Rican. Perhaps that is how he got that tad of Spanish flavor in his accent. Yitzchak was a tiny bit taller than me but had the broad build of that of a bull. He had a very handsome, masculine face with wavy light brown hair.

Once I got to know him better, I started to like him. He was funny, silly, and liked silly jokes like I do. Yitzchak loved excitement and he somehow trusted me with driving his mini-van while I had never driven a car before. One time I was so sick and tired of him scolding me for my driving that I just let go of the steering wheel. He took over quickly while laughing about it. That was Yitzchak, not scared of anything, just of himself. Once we got to know each other better we both knew that the time for the next step in our relationship was around the corner. This would be an engagement. That would be the norm and pretty much expected in the communities we were part of. Yitzchak started to introduce me to everyone, this Rabbi, that friend, this acquaintance, that neighbor, looking for approval from everybody. This turned me off. It is as if he was looking for someone to disapprove. If he was seeking approval from his parents and his Rabbi, then I would understand, but it seemed like he was seeking approval from random people who he did not know well, just slightly. And after all that, he still was not sure if he should pop the question. One of the people he wanted me to meet was a Yemenite Rabbi from Israel, Rabbi Bashiri. Rabbi Bashiri lived in Manhattan with his wife Ronit and their four gorgeous children. The first time I saw Rabbi Bashiri, I could immediately sense the great wisdom he possessed. I started to attend Rabbi Bashiri's classes as well at night. He would give these classes to a large group of young people in his apartment at crazy hours at night until dawn. I would often fall asleep and his words of wisdom would play a role in my dreams. When I woke up, he would say with his loud Israeli accent, "Sara, there are 24 hours in a day, eight hours for sleeping, eight hours for you to do whatever you want, and eight hours for learning Torah!" However, he would always let me sleep. So, I asked, "Why didn't you have any of the women wake me up then?" He would say something like, "We cannot change the world. We can only change ourselves." Well, what can I answer to that? He seemed to have derived everything he said from the Torah somehow.

I grew closer to Rabbi Bashiri's family, especially his youngest daughter, Yael. He had a small restaurant as well and I started working for him. I was very grateful for that job as I hadn't had a job since babysitting Mr. and Mrs. Jansen's baby. I took phone orders in the evening and prepped the food in the afternoon for all the evening orders. The restaurant was kept very clean. Rabbi Bashiri respected hygiene and the quality of the food that he was selling to his customers. Everything was checked carefully for bugs and prepared with diligence. This made me respect him even more. I learned a lot about *kashruth* (regulations of a kosher diet) at his restaurant. He was pleasant to have around as well. Whenever I did or said something, he always taught me something Torah-based and positive. His words of wisdom played a significant part in shaping the person I am today.

Rabbi Bashiri and me on my wedding day.

Yitzchak was playing around; he was not willing to commit. I had to end it and move forward. Rabbi Bashiri gave me a lot of work on purpose. Working so much and so hard kept my mind off Yitzchak. "Being inactive can make one destructive" Rabbi Bashiri would say. I spoke to Rabbi Bashiri about Yitzchak and what his intentions could be. Rabbi Bashiri said, "Yitzchak is molded in a certain way. Just move on." This response opened my eyes a lot more. I thought, "Yes, I can see that." I must admit that it was difficult to just forget about him. He was a lot of fun, but I was looking for much more than just "having fun." Yitzchak kept asking for another chance which I gave him despite Rabbi Bashiri's advice. "If you were my daughter, I would break your legs so you cannot go to see him," Rabbi Bashiri would say. Every time I agreed to date Yitzchak again, it never seemed to go anywhere. He would soon go back to clowning around. I started to wonder what in the world was wrong with this dude. It seems like he can't live without me, but won't commit either. Maybe his ego just wanted to test me to see if he could still get me back whenever he wanted. Everything he tells me about his past, his family and friends sounds so perfect. He was once married to a gentile and had two children with her. Yitzchak would always talk horribly about her, how she kept their children away from him, how she would verbally abuse him etcetera. "Poor guy," I thought. I decided to ask around and dig deeper into his background.

With my earnings working at the restaurant, I was able to move to a small studio apartment on the Upper East Side of Manhattan. I was on cloud nine! I had a pizza place below me, Starbucks next to my building, a grocery store right next to Starbucks, and a Laundromat right across the street. I had everything I needed right at the tip of my fingers, except for the train. The nearest train station was on 86th Street at Lexington Avenue, which was about four Avenue blocks away. My apartment was on the second floor of a small building on York Avenue. It had a small kitchenette, a bathroom, and three large windows looking out over the avenue. You could hear all the typical New York City traffic noises inside the apartment. I absolutely loved it. Every day I would walk from my apartment on the Upper East Side to my job at the restaurant on the Upper West Side. I noticed that during rush hours, I would arrive on the Upper West Side around the same time as the cross-city bus would arrive. Yes, traffic was that dense. I would walk to Rabbi Weis's classes and events on the Upper West Side as well. I got deeply involved with the organization and volunteered sometimes.

One afternoon when I was there, I was asked if I would like to work at their front desk and do some light administrative work in the office a few days a week. I was surprised. "They want me with my limited English?" I was thinking in my head but of course did not ask them that out loud. "Sure, I would love to!" I began answering phone calls and doing some data entry. In the evenings, I would still work in Rabbi Bashiri's small restaurant. As time went on, I worked more and more for Rabbi Weiss and less at the restaurant. A few weeks later, I worked full-time for Rabbi Weiss and stopped working at the restaurant.

Every phone call that came in was answered by me first. Our community consisted mostly of young modern Jewish people who wanted to connect with other young Jewish people and learn more about Judaism. Therefore, we often received phone calls with questions related to Jewish laws. People asked all sorts of questions: "I just got my first apartment; how do I make my kitchen kosher?" "How do I hang up my mezuzah? Can I hang it up myself? Do I have to say a prayer?" "Can I somehow cook meat in a milk oven?" "Can I unplug my crock-pot on Shabbat?" "Can I flush the toilet on Shabbat?" "Why can I flush the toilet on Shabbat but not turn off the light then?" As these questions came in, and me being on my mission to find answers, I too started to learn more and more about Judaism. My knowledge in Judaism became deeper and deeper and I sometimes felt like a little Rebbetzin on the phone. I would explain about "*halachah*" (Jewish laws) to people and tell them what to do, how to fix something, where to get something, and which Rabbi to contact for specific needs such as conversions. I would set up people and families for Shabbat meals as well. With all this, I noticed myself growing more and more religious as well. One day I looked at myself in the mirror and thought, "My goodness, you have become one orthodox *yidene*." (Jewish woman)

Every week I would call around to see which families could host our young members for a meal. This way, I got to know many families as well and would sometimes visit them on Shabbat myself. I was sometimes the "spectacle" at the Shabbat tables. I often heard, "Wow, you are from Holland! You sing opera? Can you sing something for us? We will send the men away!" In the more Orthodox communities, it is considered to be immodest for women to sing in front of men. "Sara, this is my special friend and daughter of Rabbi "Huppeldepup" from Eretz Yisroel. I told her all about you! Could you please tell us your beautiful story again?"

Sometimes I just simply refused depending on my mood or if I had already told my story in that household before. Sometimes I had the feeling that I was invited merely to entertain. I would often joke that I would send a bill after Shabbat.

Being black and Hasidic

I started to get to know the Jewish communities in Brooklyn because I would go there often to get kosher groceries. Kosher groceries in Manhattan were much more limited and expensive, so I often took the train to Brooklyn for that. I started to feel more out of place in the Manhattan Jewish community and more at home in Brooklyn. I felt that the Jewish community in Brooklyn was more connected to me, my Jewish roots, and my spirit. It was all more soothing, homey, and familiar to me, even though it was obvious that Hasidic Jews in general are much more hesitant to open up to a person like myself because I am a person of color, not from a Hasidic community, and just different in general. But this never swayed me. I noticed that Hasidic teenagers often liked the idea of a colored religious person. In addition, they tend to respect me a lot, they are very careful not to insult me, be the first to help me with heavy bags or whatever, and tend to my children with such a passion. Perhaps it is just because of the way they are raised. When Hasidic teenagers speak to me in Yiddish, especially boys, they speak naturally, and they expect and fully trust that I understand everything they say without hesitation. Their words come out fast and natural, just like how they speak to their mothers. Whereas when I talk to Hasidic adults, especially women who don't know me well, they sometimes tend to speak slightly slower, more carefully, and with extra articulation, with expressions on their faces that say, "Let's see if she really understood what I just said," which is super annoying.

I genuinely don't feel less Jewish than any other Jew, and I claim my rights and position as a Jewish woman and a Jewish mother within the Jewish community. Even though it sometimes may be challenging to be a Jewish woman of color, I feel blessed and honored that God trusted me and gave this huge challenge to me, trusting me to handle my Jewish identity with pride, dignity, and grace. I know that there are many more religious women of color like myself, it is rather rare to see and experience a Jewish-born woman of color who speaks Yiddish and comes from Hasidic ancestors. Other Hasidic Jews often have a biased yet obvious idea about themselves of what a Hasidic Jew looks like. And when you look like me, it is assumed that you must have converted, because "how else can a person with your color be Jewish?"

Whenever I am outside my house in my community, especially at celebrations, somebody is always watching and observing my every move. Someone is always judging me. Sometimes I also feel that others expect me to prove myself.

Imagine being an African hunter but having the complexion of a Caucasian person. You are dressed in African hunting gear, and you are walking around in Africa in a "hunters' village," where they have never seen a person with a

Caucasian complexion. Yet, you are them; you dress like them and speak their language, and your children somehow look just like them while you look different. You walk around the village with your children, who are constantly saying "Mamie this, Mamie that" while holding on to you. You speak that African language to your children, and your children answer you. Your children are the same color as they are, but you and only you have the complexion of a Caucasian person. Can you imagine how everyone would stare at you, then at your children, and then at you again? Can you imagine how people would constantly and shamelessly stare at you and often whisper? Imagine the thoughts that are running through their minds. This is pretty much what I experience every day.

Sometimes people even take pictures secretly. And I know this because often these pictures come back to me sooner or later. When I was much younger, it could happen that I just got sick and tired of the constant staring. Once in a while, when I was in one of those moods of being sick and tired of being stared at all the time, and a Hasidic man or men would be the ones staring at me, I would say in Yiddish "What are you looking at? You know that it is inappropriate to stare at a woman." They would almost faint whenever I did this. And if a woman looked at me, I'd put one hand in my waist, sigh, and ask in Yiddish, "Can I help you with something or something? Do you want to ask me something?" Though I only did this when I was in a really bad mood, usually I would ignore others. Despite all the stares, I am treated with kindness and respect.

Henya Lederman

I had a friend who I met through other friends in Manhattan. Her name was Henya Lederman, a blonde young lady with typical Eastern European features. Henya was different and sort of an outcast herself within her own Hasidic family. She was vegan, and she had interesting obsessive habits that often seemed silly and unhealthy to me. She had very strong, extreme liberal political views and opinions. I mean, she would completely boycott you out of her life if you dared to agree one ounce with any republican philosophy. Her roommates changed all the time, and she was always in heated feuds with any roommate she had at the time. Henya was one of my closest friends. She was two years older than me and not yet married, which did not surprise me. It would take a miracle to find a man who would live up to the long and unrealistic checklist she had of what her husband must be like, how he must think, and what he should and should not have. She did not have many other friends either, as Henya seemed to have issues with many. I did notice that she could hold pleasant conversations better with men than with women.

One Sunday morning, she asked me to join her in baking cookies at her aunt's house in Brooklyn. I know that she did not use her own kitchen because she did not trust her roommates to abide by her strict rules for keeping the kitchen kosher. On top of that, her cookies had special gluten-free ingredients and certain amounts of a specific type of sugar. Her oats had to be ground to a specific size as well, so it was not like she would just go to a store and buy cookies there.

"Baking cookies? Americans bake cookies?" I thought. I was surprised. In Holland, we bake all the time. If you went to a store in the village where I am from, the baked goods would mostly be wholesome and made from scratch to a certain level. The chance that your cookies or breads were prepared in a factory was small. I always baked all sorts of cookies, apple pies, and cakes as a child. "Of course, I will join you!" I responded excitedly.

We arrived in Brooklyn at Henya's Hasidic aunt Chanshie's house in a very religious Hasidic neighborhood. I knew very little about this neighborhood, but the energy immediately felt comfortable and familiar to me. I also got along very well with her aunt from the get-go, as if we knew each other from before. Her aunt was big on baking too. She would always bake all the cakes, cookies, and other goodies for her grandchildren's *bar* or *bat mitzvah* (the Jewish "coming of age" ritual), or *upsherin* (the hair-cut ceremony for when a boy turns three) and Jewish holidays.

"I did not realize that Americans are so fond of baking," I said to her.

"Oh yeah, sure! Most *heimishe* (like home/unpretentious) women bake all the time!" Chanshie responded.

One Shabbat I had lunch at the penthouse of a very wealthy Jewish family in Manhattan. Their two children, their partners, and their children were there as well. The grandfather was talking to his, I believe, five-year-old grandson during lunch, testing his knowledge with various questions. At some point during their conversation, the grandfather explained to his grandson how to make pancakes, starting with where all the ingredients come from.

"First the farmer gets milk from the cow," he said.

His grandson interrupted him, "No *zeyde* (Yiddish word for grandfather)! Milk does not come from a cow. It comes from the store!"

I almost fell out of my chair. The spoiled behavior of some Manhattan kids around me and this statement of this little boy really made me believe for a long time that those rich kids from Manhattan knew nothing about the basics of life, animals, and nature. They just seem to know about trips to Israel and the Hamptons, nannies, baby gym, and Tots Shabbat. Maybe also the Wholefoods store, but what does that mean to them? How can they appreciate what they consume when they know nothing about how it's produced? Today, I understand that this was of course rather incidental.

Aunt Chanshie had six children: three older sons and three younger daughters. Five of her six children were already married. Only her youngest daughter, Chavie, was 16 or 17 years old and not yet married. Aunt Chanshie and her husband Yisroel were both the children of Hungarian Holocaust survivors. They were kind, simple, and absolutely drama-free. Aunt Chanshie had a high-pitched voice and spoke a lot. She was very mellow and not easily offended. She always made me feel very much at home and even trusted me with the access code to her front door at some point. I was extremely grateful to have found her, as her house became my heimische family home away from home.

My first Shabbat there was on a beautiful sunny Friday. I had just had a shower, and I was standing at the front door opening in my long black velour *Shabbat* robe, just chatting with her daughter-in-law and watching the men in their long black silk jackets called "*beketche*" and their high fur round hats called "*shtreimel*" on their way to the different synagogues in the neighborhood. I just kept watching. The energy in the air felt so true to my spirit. At some point, Aunt Chanshie came and joined us; she thought that this was all new to me and was worried that I might feel overwhelmed or out of place. I reminded her that I was from Europe and that I lived only two hours away from Antwerp, where we have Hasidim as well. I also told her that my great-grandmother came from a Belzer mother. I became slightly annoyed. I wondered if she would feel the same if she had a guest who wasn't of color.

Moving to Brooklyn

I continued attending Rabbi Weis's classes and events. I started having a solid small circle of friends, which grew larger and larger, and so did my knowledge in Judaism. Every Shabbat was spent with a group of people in Manhattan. I had one friend, Dalia. She was an opera singer like me, and she lived on the Upper West Side with two other roommates, Esther and Shannon. Sometimes we would spend Saturday afternoons together, along with some Stern college friends. We would have the happiest time just talking about nonsense while eating and later falling asleep on each other's shoulders like sisters would. As everybody got married and moved away one by one, we grew apart.

Even though I lived in Manhattan, I did my grocery shopping in Brooklyn. One day I entered a *Judaica* store, which is a store that sells Jewish art, spiritual items, and books. I wanted to buy some new candle sticks for lighting the Shabbat candles. Behind the counter was a Hasidic young man named Joely.

"Can I help you with something?" he asked.

"I am looking for nice *Shabbos* (shabbat) candle sticks," I responded.

Every time I needed something, especially books to learn more about a certain topic, I would go to this same Judaica store, and Joely or one of his parents would be working. Joely would often help me choose which book I should purchase based on what topic or which Rabbi wrote it. He would often speak Yiddish to others, sometimes about me but of course not realizing that I could understand every word. His gossip was always positive though. One time he mentioned my beauty to another gentleman in the store.

As I spent more and more time in Brooklyn, I felt more at home there than in Manhattan, and decided to move there. I found a lovely small and cozy one-bedroom apartment. The apartment was situated a few steps below ground level. Once you enter the apartment, you find yourself in the spacious kitchen; further toward the back, there are two rooms next to each other, a large and a smaller room. I used the smaller room as my bedroom and the larger room as my living room. Between the rooms and the kitchen, there was a hallway, the staircase to go to the basement, and the bathroom.

One day I went to the Judaica store to get a nice door plaque with my name on it so everyone would know that I lived there. Joely was working.

"Hi Joely, how are you?" I said. "I need a door plaque with my name on it for my new apartment here in Brooklyn."

"Ooh, you moved? So nice!" he responded. "Okay, what is your last name and how do I spell it?"

I didn't even know how to pronounce my last name in English. "Uh...it's van Scheffer... V-a-n-s-c..."

"No, I meant in Hebrew," Joely interrupted. "How do you spell it in Hebrew? Or do you want it in English?" he asked.

I wanted my name in Hebrew but had no idea how to spell it in Hebrew. I wrote it down in Dutch, then asked him to translate it into Hebrew. I guess that the interesting

Dutch last name together with my past purchases of random books and Jewish paraphernalia made Joely very curious about me.

He asked, "Where are you from? Who are you? What is your life story?"

Usually, Hasidic men don't hold unnecessary conversations with women other than their mother, wife, daughter or sister. Even though Joely was Hasidic, did not speak any English until his teens, and came from a very strict Hasidic family, he happened to be super social, friendly and naturally more open-minded. When he spoke to me or when I spoke to him, he often looked directly into my eyes.

During this long conversation, he found out that I speak and understand Yiddish. Joely started to blush realizing that I understood everything he said about me in the past few months. Soon he became like a brother to me. We could talk to each other about anything and laugh or cry about it without feeling the weight or pressure of how appropriate or inappropriate our conversations might be. They were always raw, honest and never sugar-coated. I never felt the need to use a filter when speaking with him, and I don't think he does either. I got to know his wife Mindy as well who was just as laid back as her husband. I went to their house often to spend time with them and their children on Shabbat. Joely volunteered for a private Jewish civilian patrol organization. He knew everyone and everything in the community. If he did not know something and wanted or needed to know, he could find out with one phone call. So, I asked him to make some findings about Yitzchak. I gave Joely all the information I had to start a small investigation.

Joely with my second son Moishe.

The next time I went to the store, Joely gave me some shocking information about Yitzchak.

"Sara, Yitzchak is still legally married to his supposed ex-wife." I could not believe it. I spoke to his uncle's Rabbi. Doesn't his wife live in Westchester? Isn't her name Yvette? Doesn't he have two children with her? They are separated but not legally divorced yet."

I walked out of the store upset. I did not want to believe Joely. However, now in the back of my mind, it did all make sense why Yitzchak would refuse to commit to me. I wanted to find out more. Yitzchak loved to tell me all about how horrible his ex-wife was. He told me how she was manipulating their children and how she was lying to their friends and family so that they would side with her. "Maybe I should look into that further" I was thinking.

There was this one family friend who was helping his wife, about whom Yitzchak always complained. She was the widow of a famous singer and very wealthy. She owned a large estate in New York. And since her late husband was so famous, it should not be so difficult to track her down. I started searching for her on the internet and found out that she had started a non-profit organization for domestically abused women. "How ironic," I thought.

I contacted the organization and explained that I needed to speak to her and why. She called me back later that day. After I introduced myself and explained the situation between me and Yitzchak, she laughed in disbelief at the "absurdness of it all," as she called it, especially when I told her the story that Yitzchak told me about his wife. She confirmed as well that Yitzchak is still legally married.

"Is it okay with you if I pass your number on to his wife, Yvette? Perhaps she should tell you her side of the story herself," she said.

I received another phone call that evening while at the movies with Esther and some Stern College girls. When I realized it was Yvette, I stepped out and missed the whole movie to hear what she had to say. Yvette had a high-pitched voice with a very heavy and sharp Hispanic accent. She was from Peru. Her voice and especially her laugh reminded me of that of a witch from Dutch cartoons I used to watch as a child on television. Yvette told me absolutely everything about Yitzchak, from Yitzchak's childhood to the moment she and Yitzchak met to when she gave birth. She also told me what was happening between them at the time. She poured it all out. I could sense she was a dramatic person right away; her voice was just loaded with passion for anger, and she was so eager to convince me to hate Yitzchak as much as she did, she even cried several times during the conversation. They were together for twelve years and she explained that Yitzchak was verbally, mentally and physically abusive to her. She told me that he had neglected their children several times, and he was neglected as a child by his "crazy" mother himself. She told me she had police reports to prove everything. In addition, she had a video recording of when Yitzchak drove over her toes with his car in their driveway.

All this information was just way too much for me—way too much to process in one evening, and everything was so incredibly negative and unnecessary for me to learn. I did not care to see police reports or video footage; I knew enough and stopped entertaining the idea of dating Yitzchak again. When Yitzchak learned about my call with his wife and her friend, he begged and told me that everyone was lying about him. "Why do you believe these *goyim* (Gentiles) over me?" he said. Even if his wife was lying, I didn't want to deal with all the drama surrounding his life in the first place.

I quickly adjusted to my new life in Brooklyn and fell in love with it. I felt right at home and lived right in between a Hasidic neighborhood and a Litvish/Yeshivish neighborhood. The place felt like neutral ground, with no specific affiliations. A lot of Hasidic Jewish and non-Jewish Eastern Europeans lived there, especially Russians and Uzbeks, and some *Yeshivishe* families. I had the vast Hasidic neighborhood on the west, the wealthy Syrian neighborhood directly south and east, the Litvish and Yeshivishe neighborhood starting a few blocks further south and east, and the Sefardi/Israeli community on the south. *Litvishe* Jews are Jews originating from Lithuania, and they are non-Hasidic orthodox Jews, often with strong connections to the orthodox Yeshiva world.

My landlords were a middle-aged modern Hungarian Jewish couple with one son and one daughter who were teenagers at that time. The mother's name was Janka; she was a heavy-set lady with glasses over a round face and short, dark, wavy hair, which she only covered on Shabbat or a Jewish holiday. Janka had quite a heavy Hungarian accent; she moved to the United States as a teenager. Janka was kind, always smiled, and loved to have a chat. She absolutely loved it. If I ran into her, I knew that I was about to lose at least 30 minutes of my time, as it was never a simple "hi and bye" with Janka; she always wanted to *schmooze*. (chat)

Janka often surprised me with homemade Shabbos treats. Her husband, Janoz, was a simple, hardworking, and very kind man with a kind heart. He was always ready to help anyone. They were kind people, but super nosy. There was a washing machine and dryer in the basement, which I was allowed to use. So, I often ran into them or their children. Their children were shy and did not say much, unlike their parents. If I asked their children something, they would always answer in an uncertain tone. Many of my immediate neighbors were Jewish and observant in the same way that my landlords were. Many were middle-aged, children of Holocaust survivors, modern Orthodox, with no more than four children and no more than twelve grandchildren. Here and there, I had a Haredi neighbor.

Me, right after I moved to Brooklyn.

The Gestetners

In Manhattan, at work, we had a student, and his name was Tom Grun. Tom was a short, skinny young man with dark curly hair and glasses who was modern-orthodox, and super pro-Israel. He was always very happy and overly positive. He had Orthodox relatives and they lived close to me in Brooklyn. He brought me into contact with them. My first impression was how posh and perfect they were. If I had to imagine a movie about Europe and the movie had to show a wealthy, posh Jewish European family, I would picture Tom Grun's family. Their house was also spotless, and they had a cleaning lady around most of the time.

Mr. and Mrs. Mordechai and Mimi Grun. They had four children, of which two were married and had children themselves. I looked at their wedding pictures and they were just so very perfect. Everything, from the wedding flowers to the dresses to the hair styles, and the absolutely perfect and artistic color coordination of it all, the whole thing was beyond flawless.

While I was looking at a family picture of one of those weddings, Mrs. Grun explained to me that, even though the bride and the groom were in the picture, it was actually taken before the *chuppah* ceremony (a Jewish wedding ceremony held underneath a traditional nuptial canopy). I looked at her, mortified. In Orthodox Jewish traditions, a bride and a groom are not supposed to see each other or speak to each other the week prior to their wedding. The first time they will see each other is during the wedding, when the groom veils the bride.

"What do you mean by saying this picture was taken before the *chuppah* ceremony?" I asked surprised.

Mimi laughed. Despite being very Orthodox, she was able to appreciate the humor in something that happened or was unintentionally done in violation of Jewish laws. She responded, "The photographer has a computer program he uses to cut the bride and groom from another picture and put them in this picture."

"Okay...." I responded, still confused. "Why all that trouble if he can just make a picture of the whole family together after the *chuppah*?"

Now Mimi looked mortified at me. She responded, "Getting the whole family together right after the *chuppah*, including all the children, and making time to have them all pose perfectly for pictures? No, there is no way! There is no time for that! Do you know how long it takes to get a good picture in which everyone poses somewhat acceptable?"

"Oh my" I was thinking. Mimi got a little worked up. I wondered if I had just said something ridiculous. It sounded so simple to me, but I guess I was wrong. No wonder her house, weddings, lunches, and dinners were perfectly organized. It was clear that Mrs. Mimi Grun was "wearing the pants" in that house. She ran a tight ship, making everything appear and sound so simple and effortless until you learn about all of her thoughts and progress behind everything she organizes.

It was Passover 2006, and I was at Mr. and Mrs. Grun's house again for lunch. Mr. Grun's sister was also there with her husband and the children that were not yet married and still living at home. It was a lovely spring day, and I was standing in the doorway of the Grun family's lovely home in the middle of Midwood Brooklyn, as if it were my own house. Other families were passing by on their way home from the synagogue.

One fancy lady with bright red lipstick, a red curly wig, and super uncomfortable heels stood still in front of the house. She pointed at me and said, "Sara?" I glanced at her while thinking "oh no, I must have forgotten her face. Who is this, who is this?" wondering where I had met her before. Before I could answer her, she walked up the six steps with her hand extended and said, "I am Tova, Tova Gestetner. I am Tom's cousin. He told me so many amazing things about you!"

Tova had that typical New York "Jewish mother" way of talking with that typical Brooklyn accent. She introduced me to her two daughters and her daughter-in-law. Tova had more children who were married and had other plans that day for lunch, I suppose. Her daughters were super sweet and polite, and one of them was nearly flawless. It was obvious that physical appearances were very important to this family. We all sat down and started *schmoozing* (chatting). They talked about different people, who got engaged, who did what, who said what, who had a baby and so on. They seemed to know everyone in Jewish Brooklyn. Once all the cousins and aunts were updated on what was going on with who, their attention was shifted back to me. The questions started pouring in.

"So Sara, I hear you are from Holland. What brought you to New York? How do you like New York? Is there a

Jewish community in Holland? So, wait, your mother is Jewish? So you were born Jewish than! Where is your mother from?"

Like a broken record, I answered all the questions and told them about my Jewish background once again. The family was amazed, but more by how I picked myself up and moved to New York, than by my unusual Jewish background. Especially Tova's nearly flawless daughter, who was so skinny, sweet, pretty, strawberry-blonde, and soft-spoken. She showered me with compliments.

After a while, all the husbands and sons came back from the synagogue. They all greeted me nicely with "*Gut yontiv!*" (Happy holiday) They all told me their names but two minutes late, I really had no idea anymore who was who. Everyone sat down at the table hungry. Next to the youthful Tova was a big, tall, older gentleman with a thick, long gray beard, big glasses, and a black hat. He looked a lot older than Tova, and I tried to figure out what their relationship was. They sat next to each other, which is supposedly not appropriate unless they are married or he is her older brother or something. It turned out that he was Tova's husband after all. His name was James Gestetner. He did not go by his Jewish name.

Tova had three more sons, one of whom was married. Her sons were all goofy, especially the middle son. They had a real silly sense of surreal humor; they said the wildest things that made absolutely no sense just to get a certain shock reaction out of somebody. Their mother, Tova, could not relate to her sons in this way, and neither could their sisters, who would mostly just ignore the "stupidity" of their brothers altogether, unless it was really inappropriate, and then they would tell them to stop. I did notice their father James carefully listening, enjoying and giggling at his son's jokes several times. They must have gotten this sense of humor from their father. James did not say much, but you could see his mind running. He always listened carefully to what was being said around him, especially if it was something embarrassing, funny, or exciting. He always had a slight grin on his face. I visited the Gestetners on a regular basis and got to know them well.

Mrs. Mimi Grun and me dancing at her son's wedding.

The wedding of the Gestetner's almost-perfect daughter was the first wedding I attended in New York. She got engaged to a guy who was almost as perfect as she was, and he had a gazillion sisters who ironically looked similar to his bride. The wedding was in a beautiful hall in Queens, New York. It was a round ballroom with glass walls. I was wearing a dusty pink skirt and matching blouse, and I had my camera with me. Besides the Gruns and the Gestetners, I did not know anyone at this wedding. Tom was there as well, but the men and women were separated, so he was on the men's side. After the *bedeken* ceremony (veiling of the bride), I sat at a cocktail table, processing the *bedeken* ceremony. Tova and her daughters were all so emotional. Those tears did not go well with their beautiful dresses, hair, and makeup, but it was nice to see this emotional side of them.

I was abruptly disturbed by a young Hispanic gentleman, the waiter. "Hi, may I ask you something?" he said.

"Sure," I responded.

"What are you doing here?" he asked me.

I didn't know how to respond to his stupid question that stemmed from his biased idea of what a guest at an Orthodox Jewish wedding looks like. I decided to act really animated and give him a stupid answer.

"Oh, I was just passing by and could hear all the jolly music from outside, so I thought, 'Oh! There must be a Jewish wedding going on and they must have food!' So I came here to sit and eat."

He looked at me and asked, "Do you know the family of the bride or groom?"

I shrugged my shoulders. "No, I don't know anyone," I answered in a comically nonchalant way, with my eyes wide open like a clueless child.

He probably realized that I was messing with him, so he walked away. I was a bit agitated for a while because of what the waiter asked me. However, this feeling disappeared quickly once the room started to fill up with heavy sacred energy.

The *chuppah* ceremony was about to start. The lights were turned off except for the ones by the *chuppah*. As the bride slowly approached, fully veiled, the groom seemed to be connected with a higher spirit while standing under the *chuppah*, swaying back and forth on the beat of the slow, solemn music with his eyes closed. We could only see the bride's face for a slight moment when her veil was lifted to take a sip from the silver cup of wine or grape juice.

"*Mazel Tov!*" (Good luck/congratulations) everybody said out loud. The couple are now officially husband and wife according to Jewish law.

The dinner was fancy, and the music was a mixture of typical Jewish wedding music with a twist or beat of more modern, totally non-Jewish dance music here and there. "What a beautiful wedding," I thought. The perfect strawberry-blonde Gestetner *kallah* (bride) was beaming radiantly. From then on, I got invited to all the Gestetner and Grun *simchas* (celebrations).

My infamous friends

At the wedding of the youngest son of Mordechai and Mimi Grun, when I arrived at the wedding hall, all the way down at the bottom of the staircase stood a Hasidic family who seemed to be completely out of place. They stood there in a tight pack, obviously uncomfortable, waiting for something. It was a father who was wearing a low furry hat with a very wide brim, a long silk black jacket called a *beketche*, white long socks, and above that, a pair of black pants that looked like three-quarter pants. The mother looked like the perfect Hasidic mother, just as the pictures of Hasidic mothers in Hasidic children's story books show. She was shorter, had glasses, a modestly colored headscarf, which we call a *tichel*, and a stiff, dark-colored suit with heavy black stockings. Her heavy-set daughter and daughter-in-law were dressed very similarly to her, and her married son and her daughter's husband were dressed similarly to her husband. Then they had two teen-aged sons, about five grandsons, two granddaughters, and a daughter who was approximately twelve years old at that time.

All the unmarried girls were wearing white stockings and very frumpy, shapeless, old-fashioned dresses or skirts with light-weight jackets or blouses, and they all had two braids in their hair. They just stood there as I descended the staircase, slowly taking it all in and wondering who they were. I Basically did what I don't like what people do to me all the time.

I was almost down when the mother of the pack made eye contact with me and smiled politely. I smiled back, and she said, "You must be Sara. I've heard so many nice things about you."

Now I was even more curious and confused. I must have been frowning. Now the rest of her daughters and daughters-in-law were smiling too.

"Yes, I am. How do you know? Who are you?" I asked.

"My name is Zeldy Grun, and my husband, Yaakov Grun, is the older brother of Mordechai Grun and Tova Gestetner."

I was so surprised. I thought, "What ties this ultra-Hassidic family to the most fashionable Jewish family in Midwood Brooklyn? They seem worlds apart."

Zeldy clearly noticed me being surprised but did not bother to explain the differences. She just shook her head, saying that's the way it is, and I didn't ask any questions. Zeldy's husband joined the conversation and started to talk to me by asking me questions about my Jewish background without looking at me. He looked right past me or something, or maybe at my shoulder, as Hasidic men usually don't look at women when speaking with them. He was friendly though; he was clearly a people-person.

"You have to come to our house for *shabbos* (shabbat) once," Zeldy's husband said. "Zeldy, give her our phone number," he instructed his wife in Yiddish.

Towards the end of our conversation, I asked if they would be coming into the wedding hall.

"Oh no, we are leaving already," Zeldy answered uncomfortably.

"Leaving? The wedding has barely started. Why won't you come in?" I asked.

Her husband interrupted, "We cannot go in, *mazel tov*. Enjoy yourself. With God's will, you will come to our house for *shabbos* soon. Bye." Her husband Yaacov abruptly ended the conversation, and I went into the hall.

"Interesting," I thought.

The next time I was at Mordechai and Mimi's house for shabbat, I mentioned that I had met their brother Yaacov Grun at the wedding.

Mordechai answered, "Oh, you did? That's nice."

Mimi kept quiet, her eyes glued to her soup. Their youngest unmarried daughter swiftly looked in her father's direction for a moment, wondering if he was really going to have a conversation with me about his infamous brother Yaacov Grun. It was clearly an uncomfortable topic and got quickly shifted by Mimi, who asked for the *soup mandeln,* which is a crunchy topping for soup. After that question, Mimi changed the subject further.

When Mimi was busy in the kitchen, Mordechai explained that his brother was part of a very extreme anti-Israel group. His brother met with certain Islamic leaders and did some things against the State of Israel. The family was not too happy about this, especially Mimi, who was partially Israeli, and they rarely saw him and his family because of this.

"He is a nice guy, absolutely, and if you want to spend time with them, then that is fine, but it is better not to talk about them when Mimi is around."

I was completely flabbergasted, yet super curious. I did not even know that such a Jewish group existed! Yaacov and Zeldy Grun invited me for the first days of *Pesach,* which means "Passover" in English. I traveled to Monsey, New York, where they lived. They had a large house on a private lot with a swimming pool in the backyard, which they never used. Zeldy greeted me very warmly, as did her youngest son Mendel and daughter Miriam-Hinda.

"Oh, yes, that short girl with the two braids," I thought.

Miriam-Hinda had very thick dark brown hair, dark eyes with thick eyebrows above them, and she was short for her age. She was about twelve years old but looked like a nine-year-old in a super frumpy dress. I brought the most beautiful roses for Mrs. Grun. She accepted them warmly and put them in a very pretty crystal vase right away. She instructed Miriam-Hinda to show me around and to show me where I was sleeping. Everything was covered in plastic in their house for Passover. Their couches, the cabinets and breakfront, the highchair that they used for their grandchildren—just everything. In the kitchen, they covered everything with silver foil. I literally had to blink my eyes from the light's reflections on the silver foil when I entered the kitchen. I was immediately told to wash my hands at the washing station next to the restroom, and again in the regular kitchen, and then in the Pesach kitchen before I touched anything in the Pesach kitchen, especially food and drinks. Miriam-Hinda showed me a practical twin-sized bed next to her bed, where I was sleeping. We spoke a lot of Yiddish to each other, especially if one of her brothers was involved in the conversation. This is because they really did not speak any English, just a word here and there.

Behind all that frumpiness, there were some normal, really funny kids with a great sense of humor. We had a lot of fun. I was surprised by how engaging the older teenage boy was. He even stood next to me and held onto my phone while I was still holding it, to look at something on it, almost making physical contact. I could tell that this made Mrs. Grun and even Miriam-Hinda very uncomfortable, as if they were holding their breaths. Their eyes moved quickly as they remained quiet. It would not surprise me if he purposely tried to provoke something. He should have known very well that his mother would not be happy about this. Mrs. Grun started to pay close attention and sat me and her son as far away from each other as possible during meals.

Mrs. Grun started to set the table for the *seider* (a Jewish ceremonial dinner held on Passover), and her youngest son Mendel grabbed the crystal vase with the flowers that I brought for Mrs. Grun. He sat the heavy crystal vase empathically in the middle of the table. "Boom!". Mrs. Grun went off on him, screaming for him to take it off immediately. I was standing right there, but that did not matter.

    "Nein! Nem es aroof! Ich vill nicht!" she screamed in Yiddish. "No! Take it off I don't want (it on the table)!"

    Her son asked her, "Why not? It's in celebration of Passover!"

"I do not want it!" she finally yelled.

She was nervous about the flowers not being "kosher enough" for Passover, because on Passover, we don't use anything that we would use otherwise because it could contain or have been in contact with anything that contains *chametz*. *Chametz* is a leavening agent and forbidden on Passover, and therefore Mrs. Grun was uncomfortable with the flowers on the table.

Usually, a Hasidic son of Mendel's age would not question his mother in this way, but Mendel was a little bit of a "provoker." He was easily distracted and shamelessly interrupted his father often during prayer by messing around or teasing somebody. He was very curious and was always looking into something or trying something he was not supposed to try. Of course, I was insulted by Mrs. Grun's outburst.

She immediately explained, "It is not you! Absolutely not! We are just very careful, you know?" she said. "Haha…I don't know where these flowers came from, and *chas v'shulem* (God forbid), what if they are from some deli where a *goy* (a gentile) was eating his ham-sandwich, there where the flowers were standing, you know? We don't know. You don't even know!"

I just stared at her with raised eyebrows.

She could read my face. She tutted her tongue and explained herself further. "Of course, probably not! But who knows? What if that's the case? Yuh? We don't know, right?"

I just shook my head and went on my way. Her English was so bad that she would build up words to make a sentence in

English in the exact same sequence as we would say it in Yiddish.

There was a race against the clock. Everything had to be ready before sundown, but the kitchen was in chaos. There were boxes and packages of unprepared food lying around. They made everything themselves, even mayonnaise, even candy! They barely purchased any prepared food from the store, not trusting it to be kosher enough. Miriam-Hinda and I were peeling a whole box of potatoes while Mrs. Grun was wrapping up a number of dishes for that evening. At some point, her oldest married daughter arrived to help out also.

As chaotic as things were only an hour ago, now after sundown the house was clean, calm, and quiet. All the married children, along with their spouses and children, joined for the Passover seder. All the men and boys sat at one end of the table, and the women and girls at the other end. I could feel that it was preferred for me to just stay in my seat, but at some point during the seder, Mrs. Grun and her oldest daughter were busy in the kitchen, and the approximately nine-month-old granddaughter was crying and screaming her *tuches* (her butt) off in the highchair while sliding down in it and almost falling out of the chair. I observed the scene closely without anyone saying or doing anything. Nobody was paying attention. All the sudden, the baby's father got up and walked towards his daughter but instead of grabbing his own daughter, the father passed his daughter to grab a prayer book from the break-front. I got up and walked over to where the men were sitting to take her out of the high chair. Mr. Grun kept his eyes glued to his unmarried son while I was doing this.

I was sitting in between Mrs. Grun and Miriam-Hinda all the way on the other end of the table, as far away from the men as possible. The seder went on until about 4 a.m. When we retired to bed, we saw the sun rising. As tired as we were, Miriam-Hinda and I chatted for a while before falling asleep. She explained that she was very happy that I slept in her room.

"I am sure you miss having Raizel around," I said. Raizel is her older sister who got married not too long ago, and was living with her husband and their two young children.

Miriam Hinda replied, "Raizel never slept in my room. I usually sleep in the hallway, but now that you are here, I sleep in my room."

I was surprised, so I asked her, "Why did you sleep in the hallway?"

"We have been harassed several times," she responded. "One time some people even threw rocks through my bedroom window."

I didn't know what to say. I just laid there on my back staring at the ceiling. I didn't know how much she knew about her father. Eventually I responded, "Oh wow. I am so sorry, Miriam-Hinda."

There was nothing cozy or comfortable about their house. Everything was just practical and they did everything according to how they thought it should be done. The curtains were always closed and they lit the living room up with cool dimmed ceiling lights, making it feel like a conference room in an office building. The sofa was small, shallow, stiff, and on top of that, it was completely covered in plastic. If I wanted to relax, I figured that their backyard would be the most comfortable place. I sat there a lot with Miriam-Hinda. Our conversations centered around how I grew up compared to how she was being raised, how we say certain things in Yiddish versus how you say it in Dutch, and so on.

It was nice and warm outside. I had my feet up until Mrs. Grun saw that. She explained in a very uncomfortable way that I should not sit with my feet up. She said that it was an immodest position to sit in for a woman if her husband or sons saw me.

"What if I cover my legs completely with a blanket then?" I asked Mrs. Grun.

"No, that's also not good... I'm sorry, okay?" she said as she smiled and returned inside.

At some point, I just could not wait to go back home and be comfortable. Mrs. Zeldy Grun did her best to make my stay comfortable. However, she was just so rigid in her ways that they often clashed with what I really needed to feel comfortable. Despite all this, we continued to stay in close contact, and I continued to visit them sometimes for shabbat. I did not mind spending one night with them; it was worth it to see everybody. But I would not do three-night or longer holidays anymore.

Their second oldest son also got engaged at some point. I was at their house when they made the announcement. Mrs. Grun was overjoyed. The bride was a 17-year-old girl from a small Hasidic community in North Westchester, New

York. The bride didn't fit your stereotypical beauty, but she came from a wealthy family. Mrs. Grun felt like she had hit the jackpot and did not make a secret of it. She shamelessly told her oldest daughter in Yiddish, "Her family has a lot of money, so Aryeh does not have to work. He can learn while he is married!" The bride's name was Malka, and she was the absolute sweetest young girl.

Mrs. Zeldy Grun and her daughter Miriam-Hinda on my wedding.

The other side of a perfect orthodox father.

I continued working for the non-profit organization in Manhattan while living in Brooklyn. I started to really dread my commute to work, especially in the winter months. When I left my apartment in the morning, it was still dark outside, and when I arrived back home, it was dark already. However, I felt safe there, it was a steady job that provided a steady income, and I loved the community. It was an hour and fifteen minutes to commute each way, and I dreaded riding those crowded trains twice a day during rush hours. I really appreciated Shabbat and enjoyed being in my apartment just hanging out on Sundays. One day I got a strange phone call from someone who clearly knew me. The conversation started very casually, and I was curious about who the caller was.

Further into the conversation, the gentleman started to carefully ask me questions, trying to figure out where I was standing sexually. I thought that it must be Yitzchak somehow, or he must have something to do with this. As I spoke with this person, I was firm but polite. At some point, he got comfortable enough to tell me who he was. It was James Gestetner, the father with the perfect house and family. Even though I wasn't completely surprised that he had this side to him, I was stunned that he took such a risk contacting me and asking me these questions, knowing how close I was to his family. I wondered, "Why me?"

He desperately tried to find out if I was sexually deprived, but I refused to discuss my sexual life with him. I listened to everything he had to say about his. I understood that this was highly inappropriate in the Orthodox Jewish community. However, in the Netherlands where I came from, and especially Amsterdam, sex was not considered inappropriate or taboo. Prostitution is legal there, and you can go to a children's amusement park and just run into a statue of a naked lady. Therefore, James and his stories were nothing particularly interesting or something that should or could not be discussed. Of course, today, even though I maintain that sex is not taboo, even when you are married, I should not have tried to be "the therapist" for him and discuss his sexual issues with him. I thought it was harmless at the time. He just needed someone to talk to, and in his community, finding that person who is open-minded and private enough to talk about his sexual struggles objectively would be very difficult and uncomfortable.

James felt sexually deprived and admitted to heavily cheating on his wife with a young lady who worked for him in his lingerie shop. He talked about how his wife Tova does not like to perform certain sexual acts on him or even allow him to perform them on her. Then he asked if I had ever performed those specific sexual acts on a man.

"It's really none of your business, James," I replied. "Stop asking me these questions or this conversation will end."

He apologized profusely and almost begged me not to hang up. He called me more and more often, and I first figured that these conversations were therapeutic for him, especially as he often asked for advice. At some point, he tried to bribe me to have sex with him.

"Are you seriously under the impression that that might be a possibility, James?" I snapped. "Please seek professional help and don't call me again."

"No, Sara! I am sorry! No, wait!"

I hung up the phone and blocked his number.

Weeks went by, and I did not hear from Mr. Gestetner until one day when I was sitting at my desk at work and my work phone rang. I picked up the phone and introduced myself as I usually do. Mr. Gestetner immediately informed me of who he was as he breathed heavily. In my naive mind, I wondered why he was breathing like that.

"Please say something!" he pleaded.

"What? Why? Is everything all right with you?" I asked.

All of a sudden, he started gasping, moaning, and groaning out loud. I realized what was going on and what had just happened. If I were Caucasian, my face probably would have turned completely red like a tomato. Without saying anything, I hung up the phone in shock. I was angry at myself for allowing this crazy man to use my voice for his own sexual pleasure. Uugh! I wanted to punch myself. I did not hear anything from him for a few days. At this point I was so disturbed by his actions. The next time he called me at work again, I threatened to tell his wife that he was harassing me. I never heard from him again and stopped visiting James and Tova's house on Shabbat or any other reason because I felt uncomfortable doing so. In addition, I stopped making those spontaneous phone calls to Tova letting her know that I will be joining them on Shabbat.

Weeks passed, and Tova called to invite me to dinner on Passover.

"Oh, I'm sorry, I won't be able to make it on that day," I said.

"Okay, so which day does work for you? We miss you, Sara," she said.

Passover is a week-long holiday, so I couldn't get around it. I wondered if I was being set up and mentally prepared myself for some sort of confrontation perhaps. Maybe now Tova wants to discuss my phone calls with her husband? I didn't know if she was truly clueless or not. The day I was there for a meal, James avoided eye contact while we were eating. When Tova was not in the dining room, he would glance a few times with that grin he always wears. I ignored him as much as possible. So, in front of his children and other guests, he asked:

"Where are you going for the last days of Passover, Sara?"

"Borough Park," I answered shortly.

"Oh, nice!" he said in an exaggeratedly friendly way, with his eyes wide open, his brows raised, and a big smile on his face through his big long beard, as if he wanted to tell me to loosen up a bit and not be so awkward.

Sometimes I looked at Tova, especially when she was talking to me and I just wondered if she had any idea what goes on in the mind of her husband. They are married for longer than I have existed, "you must know something or at least sense something no?" I asked her in my mind while she was talking to me. Maybe she did not want to know? I could not even hear her sometimes while all these thoughts were running through my mind. My perception was that this family, life and especially reputation was way too perfect to mess it up. It would not surprise me if Tova did indeed has an idea of what her husband has been up to or even caught him in the act, but she just simply turns her face the other way. Whatever it is, it is fine with me.

Devorah

I had this friend named Devorah who we all called Dvoire. She was born into a very strict Hasidic family, she was from the same *Hasidis* (specific Hasidic faction) as my great-grandmother. Her father was the quiet type and of course always wore his *shtreimel* on Shabbat and holidays. Her mother was rather an extrovert, blunt, talkative, some sort of gym or fitness teacher, and was constantly on the go in her sneakers. She would always wear a short brown *sheitel* (wig) with straight, heavy bangs, simply trimmed around her head. It was a little old fashioned in my opinion. It looked to me like she was wearing a *sheitel* merely for the purpose of covering her head and not necessarily to look nice in any way. She was also the only Hasidic lady I knew who wore sneakers most of the time. Devorah had one younger brother and two younger sisters, which was a lot fewer siblings than what I was used to seeing in most other Hasidic families.

Devorah was in many ways like her mother—a free spirit who loved to talk and have fun. Devorah loved being silly. She loved to laugh; she would laugh very loud while throwing herself forward as if she could not contain her body from the overwhelming laughter. She was always chipper and ready to have fun. She was about two years younger than me and still in school when we hung out. Even though I carried adult responsibilities, she reminded me that I was still a very young and silly girl. I absolutely adored her, as I could relate to her a lot. Almost all the silliness she loved, I still enjoyed as well. Devorah would often come to my house, still in her school uniform, which consisted of a long, heavy, pleated checkered skirt with thick pantyhose underneath it and a blouse on top. She had a bit of a nerdy appearance, with dark brown wavy hair up to her shoulders and glasses. At school, she had a group of friends who all liked to have fun, and they all started to like boys. Devorah's father knew that Devorah had certain "out of the box" interests and tendencies; he was keeping a close eye on her without saying much.

One time, she was at my house and lied to her father on the phone about her whereabouts. She told him that she was at Miri's house while she was at my house. Miri was Devorah's friend from school and a direct descendant of the Rebbe of a large Hasidic dynasty, which is of course huge. Miri was a stunning-looking girl, but an absolute boy-lover who loved to stir unpleasant tensions among her friends. She would throw a rock and put her hands on her back, pretending like she never threw anything. So, Devorah lied to her father, telling him that she was at that girl's house instead of mine.

"Why didn't you just tell him where you are, Dvoire?" I asked her.

"I am not allowed to be here," she said with her hoarse voice and no shame, as if it would not insult me. "Why not?" I inquired further.

"Whatever! I don't know!" she said, trying to avoid more questions.

(tongue tut) My mom is okay with it... I guess but my father (tongue tut) I don't know I guess he thinks you maybe a negative influence on me or something" I looked at her shocked in disbelief.

She sat still, processing what she just said herself, analyzing if it came out right and then trying to rectify herself by saying "(tongue tut) He never said that though! (tongue tut) I don't know! It's just what I think!"

Even though I was not completely surprised, I certainly acted as if I was totally shocked. I replied, "So wait, you are allowed to be at Miri's house, who does all these sneaky things behind her parents' backs, who actually does sees boys and feeds you all sorts of crazy information, that you are really not supposed to be exposed to, but you are not allowed at my house?"

She burst out laughing. "I know right!" she exclaimed.

Devorah tried to give it a comical turn by acting as if she found it funny, while I found it to be very twisted. Such incidents made it clear to me that it's all about how one is perceived by others in the community. I thought, "Does it even matter what reality is? What or who you really are at the core? What is her father thinking? Maybe he is scared that someone would see Devorah coming out of this 'black lady's house,' who is not from this community. He's probably wondering, 'What is this lady feeding my pure, innocent, precious Hasidic daughter? What would others think? What would they say? Who would marry her after that?' But if someone sees Devorah coming out of Miri's house, that is completely fine because it's acceptable on the surface, no matter how rotten it is at the core." This situation left a really bad taste in my mouth about her parents, her father in particular, as her mother mostly just follows him anyway.

One day, Devorah's mother called me in all excitement, explaining that she might have found a potential boy for me for a *shidduch* (a Jewish arranged marriage). I was 19 years old. I figured that I was ready for marriage and was excited about it as well.

She said "His name is Heshy. He is absolutely lovely and from a lovely family. He has many siblings. He went to this prestigious *yeshiva* (orthodox Jewish boys' college). He has never been married. He has great references. You are tall, as is he. It is really worth giving it a chance."

I thought to myself, "Wow! This sounds so perfect. He sounds like a typical heimishe cookie-cutter, perfect boy, while I am anything but the 'perfect' typical heimishe cookie-cutter Jewish girl in the Hasidic community. I am from Holland. I am different from the other girls with an open-minded mindset and approach towards life. My parents are divorced, and even worse, my father is not even Jewish! According to Devorah's father, I am a bad influence on Hasidic girls. Oh, and oh, before I forget, I have a dark complexion. So why is it that Devorah's mother would suggest me to this so-called 'perfect' family? And why did this family agree to have their son date me?" Even though I know that I deserve no less than any other Jewish girl, my shidduch profile does not appear so perfect on paper and it is very unlikely for any supposed "perfect" family to pick me to date their son out of all the available "cookie-cutter girls" out there, unless you got to know me personally and fell in love with me, then I would understand. This boy did not know me personally, and neither did his parents... as far as I know.

I figured that there must be a catch. There must be something different or maybe even wrong with him or in this family, for them to agree for their son to date me. There must be something that Devorah's mother left out. So, I asked Devorah's mother, "Why is it that they agreed for me to go out with their son? Is there something interesting going on with the boy or in that family?"

"No nothing!" she replied. "They are a wonderful family with a really nice boy. He is excellent!"

With furrowed eyebrows, I asked, "Would you and your husband let Devorah date him?"

Now all of a sudden, he was not so excellent anymore, and she responded, "In general, we would, but no, he is not exactly like us, you know? Devorah needs someone more like us."

"What is different about him?" I asked.

"He was adopted when he was a baby," she said. "His father is black and his mother is white, but this is not a reason to turn him down. He is wonderful, and his mother is the nicest lady. What do you have to lose by going out with him just one time?"

While still processing her response, I said, "Well, why do you think that he is a great match for me? Is he similar to me? Am I different?"

She was quiet for a few seconds. Then she said, "Well, you are a little different. You don't see girls from where you are from and look like you walk in Borough Park every day, do you?"

I replied, "But just because I am different because of where I am from and because I have a dark complexion does not mean that you should necessarily set me up with someone who is also different and has a dark complexion. I'm sure there are typical boys out there who want someone unique like me. Why didn't you find me a boy who's light-skinned like your son? Do you think that I am not Jewish enough because of my complexion?"

It was not that I was not willing to date someone with a dark complexion. I merely asked these questions to figure out as precisely as possible what her opinions were when it came to people with different complexions dating and marrying each other. It felt like she was against this. If she had not mentioned that Devorah would not have been allowed to go out with him, I would have instantly jumped at the opportunity without asking any questions. The fact that she said that Devorah couldn't go out with him made me detest the idea.

When I asked her why she could not find a boy with a light complexion for me, she bluntly answered, "I think that it would look funny. The contrast would be too strong, you know? This boy is still very light in color, but you would be able to connect better, you know?"

"Huh...? Connect better?" I almost fell off my chair. "Is she actually serious? Since when does skin color have anything to do with two people's compatibility? What kind of mentality is that? All sorts of people from all sorts of backgrounds with all different types of complexions connect with each other just fine. I am living proof of that, as I grew up in rural Holland, where there was practically nobody with my complexion. My dark-skinned brother has children with his European Jewish girlfriend. They have been together for a decade and a half, and they connect just fine.

That day, I turned down the entire proposal, because I believed her reasons for why he was perfect for me were unfounded. I did not want to live for and entertain such a ridiculous and biased mindset. However, it appeared at some point that turning down this potential *shidduch*, without giving it a legitimate chance, could be harmful to my friendship with Devorah and future potentials because Devorah's mother knows pretty much everyone and many like to gossip. I agreed to give it a chance.

The day I went out with Heshy, I had on a simple royal-blue dress with long sleeves, of course, and the dress fell right over my knees. My hair was up on top and down on the bottom, with a raised bump in the front, and the ends were flipped out. Moments before I was getting picked up by Heshy, I was across the street at my neighbor's house. It was about time before Heshy picked me up, so I had to rush back to my house. As the young whimsical girl I was, I ran across the street back to my house, making ballet sautés over the sidewalk curbs with my arms spread out. Then, all of a sudden, I saw this young, skinny, tall gentleman in a white shirt and black pants with a very large black velvet yarmulke staring at me. This was while I was doing all that running, twirling, and leaping. It was Heshy. He seemed mesmerized, which made me shy.

"Hey, you are Heshy, right?" I said. "I am just getting my purse. I will be right back." I was embarrassed and continued walking calmly to my apartment as if I had not leapt before.

Heshy had borrowed his parents' minivan. He came across as hyper and spoiled to me.

"So where should we go?" he asked me.

"Where should we go?" I was surprised that he hadn't figured that out in advance. He should have figured this out before he picked me up, he could have made some sort of a reservation somewhere in advance, had some plans, or at least prepared something, but he didn't. You don't just take a girl out for the first time without a proper plan in place and without even knowing where to take her. Even though I could have suggested a million places to go, I was already disappointed. I told him that I didn't know where we should go and he would just have to figure that one out.

Eventually, after ruminating on it for way too long like a kid who could not make up his mind, Heshy decided we should go to downtown Manhattan to some new building that had a nice bar where we could sit and drink something. It sounded like a plan to me. We were talking and trying to learn more about each other while driving to Manhattan.

All of a sudden, in the middle of our conversation, Heshy went completely off topic and asked me, "Are you a ballet dancer or something?"

"...No, I am not," I answered with a frown on my face. "How are you going from talking about Israel to asking if I am a ballet dancer?"

"I don't know, I was just thinking about it," he said. "That was ballet you were doing at your house, right?" he asked.

As sweet as he was, he seemed quite immature. I could not imagine him being my husband or a father to my children. Heshy did not mention anything about him being adopted, and while I was so curious about his background, I did not ask. I thought maybe it was a very sensitive subject for him. Furthermore, if he wanted to discuss that subject, he would have said something about it himself. Instead, he talked about his adoptive parents and siblings, who are his only parents and siblings. In one way, this was beautiful. It was obvious that his adoptive family loved him very much and probably never made him feel any different from their biological children. He asked me a lot of questions about the Netherlands and Amsterdam. He had never been to Europe before and was very curious about it.

Finally, we arrived in Manhattan at the building he mentioned, but the bar was closed, so we took a walk outside. It was drizzling and the sky was gray. I was already done and just wanted to return home, but he clearly was not. We wandered around Battery Park while I was wearing some very uncomfortable heels. At some point, he spotted a cool building with a glass elevator. He asked me if I would like to go in the elevator with him. We went up and down the elevator, which was a total thrill for him. He wanted to go again. Because "it was so cool". This time he went up and down the elevator by himself while I sat on a bench waiting. I thought about what Devorah's mother said about Heshy being "an excellent boy."

Now I was absolutely certain that this was not going to work for me. Even though we had similar skin colors, we couldn't connect because we were different and had different priorities and mindsets. Heshy wanted to continue playing around in Battery Park Manhattan, but I told him that I wanted to go home. The next day, I told Devorah's mother that I was not going out with Heshy again because he was not for me. She thought the reasons I gave her for not going out with him anymore were insufficient, and tried to persuade me to give it another shot. I blatantly refused.

The following day, Devorah's mother called again to inform me that Heshy's parents had contacted her and told her that Heshy would like to go out with me again. Devorah's mother felt that I really should give it one more try, but I refused. About a week later, she told me that Heshy felt like he had waited too long for my answer, and was no longer interested in going out with me. Devorah's mother clearly did not tell him the week before that I was not interested in a second date. She was probably hoping I would change my mind.

Me around the time I went out with Heshy wearing the same dress.

One day, Devorah called me way after midnight. I picked up my phone, and she was just full of energy; it sounded as if she was on something.

"Come out! I have my father's car! Come out! Let's go to the donut shop!"

I was still half asleep and asked, "Dvoire? What, what, go where?"

She burst out laughing because of my dazed response. "I don't know! Just come!"

I hung up the phone without saying anything. Seconds later, she loudly banged on my door but tried to "stay quiet" at the same time by whispering and motioning to me through the window to open the door.

I opened the door, she started laughing again and asked, "You were sleeping, right?!"

More laughter as she dropped herself onto my very large and cozy brown velvet L-shaped sofa. Even though I was so tired and still half asleep, I loved these erratic spontaneous, crazy things she always pulled. Devorah was a girl with spice and guts, regardless of the position she was in and the restrictions that her family and community put on her.

She started to talk about this, that, and the other, but I still needed time to fully wake up and didn't totally hear, nor could I completely follow her. She was all over the place with her stories.

After a few minutes, in response to her asking something about a completely different topic, I asked, "Did you just say that you came here with your father's car? What are you doing with your father's car at this crazy time? Didn't he hide it from you?" Her father was not in town for a few days and had hidden his car, so Devorah could not use it. I didn't understand this because one would think that Devorah would not dare to touch her father's car if he simply told her not to touch it, or he could have taken the keys with him instead, but whatever.

Devorah started laughing again. "My mom secretly took it out for me, so my father doesn't know." This blew my mind, but I did not ask anything else. At some point, I was wide awake but definitely was far from being in such a hyper state as Devorah was.

Devorah started telling me that she is no longer speaking with her friend Miri, the one from the *Rebbishe* family (Rabbinical family), because Miri started, supposedly on purpose, showing interest in the same boy that Devorah really likes. I had such an idea already because that boy lived around the corner from me in a gorgeous house. I had caught Miri going into his house once, and he does not have sisters around their ages, which then could have meant that she was visiting his sister or something. I never mentioned anything to Devorah though, and asked her now how she knew that Miri likes him as well.

Devorah started to explain something like, "Henchy said that Tzippy said that Tzirel said that Mirel said that Lea'la said that Elky said that Miri was using Kreindl's secret cell phone to text him. "Then, first, she denied it when I asked her, but then she had to admit it." I just cleared my throat and didn't say anything. Devorah continued venting passionately about this but did not seem to be heartbroken or anything. She just continued talking loudly as she always does, with some loud laughter here and there.

All of a sudden, she mentions that her father is looking for a *shidduch* (a match) for her. "What! Really?" This news got my full attention instantly.

I knew that Devorah's hormones were raging, and she was really longing for a relationship with a male. However, in her world, the only way to be with a male is through marriage. It looked like Devorah was ready to get married, as young as she was. She really wanted and perhaps needed it. After a while of having a deeper and more serious conversation about it, the humor kicked back in. "I do not hope that my husband's name will be BOOHRECH! Or HILLEL! Hahaha!" She exaggeratedly articulated the names, making them sound unappealing. I could not help laughing as well.

This crazy girl I adore so much; she got engaged within weeks and involved me in all her engagement party plans. But I knew very well that we would grow apart once she got married because then her life would revolve around her husband and household, and this is exactly what happened. Once she got married, we grew apart completely.

I ran into her one more time about a decade later. She looked just like her mother and was even wearing the same type of wig her mother always wore. Devorah was still as silly as she used to be, sitting in her car, stuffing her mouth with a bagel with tuna and cheese while explaining to me that she was on a diet. "You are on a diet, but you are eating a tuna melt?" I asked. She started laughing as loud as she always used to. "Okay, fine, tomorrow I will really start dieting," she responded.

We exchanged numbers and spoke for hours over the phone that same evening while her husband was learning, and her kids were sleeping. She recommended some series for me to watch through a certain streaming service. I, in return, suggested a very popular Israeli series about a *Charedi* (ultra-orthodox) family in Jerusalem, Israel, with an unmarried son who goes through all sorts of challenges within himself. Devorah was not interested in these series, calling them flat-out "boring."

I decided to look into the series she suggested, and my jaw dropped within fifteen minutes of watching the first episode. These series were about a big dysfunctional family with many children of different ages, especially teenage children. Some of them were foster children, some adopted, and some biological. These children, however, all had hidden secrets, perverse sexual desires, anger issues, drug issues, and all sorts of problems. Some acted upon them, and some tried to restrain them but then acted out in a different way.

I was surprised that Devorah found this to be a good thing to watch. But then again, in some milder way, she probably recognized herself.

Ari Glick

In the years working for the not-for-profit organization in Manhattan, I slowly got promoted to Office Manager. Even though being the Office Manager means "managing the office", I had all sorts of random responsibilities and did not mind it. I took my job seriously and felt that we were wasting a lot of money on utter nonsense. We purchased too much food for events, of which too much would end up in the garbage by Wednesday. If there was something I could do to save money, then I would often do it. So, I started to make fruit and veggie platters for our classes and events. I made cholent, which is potatoes, beans, and meat stew, for Shabbat, and I would make all floral arrangements for certain bigger events and holidays. I would take our tablecloths to the dry cleaners, re-arranged our walk-in inventory closet, went out to purchase snacks, party supplies, vases, and office supplies at the local grocery, office, and party stores.

By then, I learned that I really do not like to be confined to a desk for hours at a time. I like to move around and be creative, have a constant change of energy and scenery, and be around and work with people. Except for the daily traveling with public transportation, I loved my job. I appreciated how Rabbi Weiss trusted me and gave me the space and freedom to be creative, buy, and do what I felt needed to be purchased and done for the Foundation.

For one event, which was a large memorial gathering for the Rabbi's late mother, I went all out to set it up as perfectly and solemnly as I possibly could. I printed out a portrait of the Rabbi's mother in large poster size and hung it on the wall. While I was setting everything up, Rabbi Kaplan came down to the ballroom to have a look at what I was doing. He completely bashed my hard work, especially the large picture of the Rabbi's mother on the wall. With a gorgeous smile on his face, he called it "too much." I told him that I would only change it if Rabbi Weiss wished me to do so and not him. Shortly after, Rabbi Kaplan returned with Rabbi Weiss. Rabbi Weiss absolutely loved it and rather appreciated it. Rabbi Kaplan shrugged his shoulders, smiled, and walked off.

I dealt with a lot of caterers as well to discuss menus and place orders, especially for Shabbat dinners. There was this one fancy catering company and restaurant on the Upper Eastside that we used to order from on a regular basis.

I became good friends with their *Mashgiach*, Mr. Ari Glick. A *Mashgiach* is a Jewish person who supervises the food and its preparations in a kosher establishment to ensure that it is all kosher. Ari Glick was divorced and had two older married children and a number of grandchildren. He was about 20 years older than me, lived not too far from me in Brooklyn, and was part of the largest Hasidic sect, which counts about 20% of all Hasidim today. Ari would only speak Hasidic-Yiddish to me and had a heavy Yiddish accent when he spoke English. He was a heavy-set, loud, and jolly guy with long blonde-gray payes (side-curls), a long beard, very outspoken, and always curious. If there was something I was occupied with that he did not know about, he would want to learn about it. He was not embarrassed to walk, talk, and laugh with me in public in our own neighborhood, even though this was considered "not proper" for a Hasidic man. It was definitely not common for a Hasidic gentleman to run around, talk and laugh with a lady he was not married to, especially a lady of color with long hair and tighter-fitting clothes. My tops would often be of a tighter fit, while my skirts would be more flowing. This behavior is usually an instigator for spreading gossip. This literally could have been a reason why his children would be turned down for a *shidduch* (a marriage proposal). Though his children were married already, he waited for his children to be married first before he divorced his ex-wife.

On Shabbat, he would often pick me up on Friday nights with his *shtreimel* (traditional Hasidic fur hat) on, in his black silk *beketche*, (traditional long silk or satin jacket) and long white socks. I always decorated my home in a cozy and comfortable way with soft velvet couches, furry pillows, and rugs. The first time Ari came to visit me with our mutual friend Mindy Fischman, whom he was dating, I opened the door, and he nearly screamed, "Git Shabbos! Git Shabbos!" He sat down in my rocking chair as if he always sat there, looked around, and asked me, "What's with all the white and fuzzy stuff?" Usually, Hasidic house decor is set up in a more sterile way to keep everything organized and to be kept clean easily. Even though I am a neat freak, my house is opposite from that of most Hasidic families. Everything is cream or white in color and soft, often including many plants, rugs, and sofas, and none of it is leather. I don't like the feel of leather on my skin, and I don't like cherry wood or any other dark-colored furniture. Ari was not used to this and clearly would never go for such "impractical" décor himself.

It became a usual thing that Ari, first with, later without Mindy, would pick me up on the evening of Shabbat to make a walk. "Git Shabbos! Git Shabbos Eshes Chayil!" he would make a few steps into my house to see how I prepared everything for Shabbos while leaving the front door open, as a man cannot be in an enclosed space by himself with a woman.

I always wore my long black velvet Shabbos robe with some sort of lacy adornments on it. I love lace and pearls. We would take long walks merely as friends, but he would talk and argue with me as if I was his wife.

He was married before and explained that he regretted marrying his ex-wife pretty much right away because she was "mentally ill". Giving the excuse that somebody is "mentally ill" is often used by divorced Hasidim, while in my opinion, the "mentally ill" person is often just simply different. One time when his children were babies, he claimed that his ex-wife left the babies by themselves across the street while she was running away from a dog. He waited until his children were married before he divorced her because it is more difficult to find a good *shidduch* for children if the parents are divorced.

Sooner or later, Ari brought up the topic of me looking for a *shidduch*. Carefully and for the first time speaking in a soft and low tone, he asked if I would consider him as a potential *shidduch*. I was shocked that he suggested this.

"You? Don't be silly; you are much older than me; I am nearly the same age as your daughter!"

Ari, with his big mouth, did not find this to be an issue at all and was deeply insulted. Now almost screaming, he asked me in Yiddish, "So? Hello, excuse me! Do you know how many *tzadikim* (righteous men) had much younger wives? And even more than one wife? Do you know how many! My age means that I am not capable of being a good husband or something? What do you think? You would be the first one to marry someone a little older than you!"

I didn't say anything back as I noticed that he was on a rant. Whatever I would say now would probably be "wrong," and he would just talk right over me. The expressions of other passersby were priceless, totally confused about what to make out of this spectacle of this heavy-set Hasidic man raising his voice in Yiddish to this young Black lady who has a mellow and care-less look on her face. I just let him rattle on for some time, trying to convince me how normal a 20-year age gap is until he would all of a sudden say, "Fine! Whatever! *Vus nuch*? (What else)? I saw that you ended up using small white beans in your cholent like I told you." And he would switch topics just like that.

If you heard Ari ranting the way he was with his loud voice, you would think he was upset, but he was really not, just rather passionate, outspoken, and insulted yes. He has absolutely no filter, everything came right out.

One afternoon, Ari called me and asked if I wanted to go to a big *Rebbishe wedding* (a wedding within a Rebbe's family) "with him". At Hasidic weddings, men and women are kept completely separate, so I wondered why he wanted me to go "with him." I didn't know anyone there and would stick out like a sore thumb being different from everyone else. Ari explained that the youngest daughter of his *Rebbe*, the *Rebbe* of his specific Hasidic faction, was getting married to the best student of his *Yeshiva*. He laughed a little and rephrased it again in Yiddish, "He just took his best student for his own daughter!"

"But what am I going to do there, Ari? I didn't get an invitation and really have no business going to this wedding," I said.

Ari answered, full of confidence as always,

"Eh! What invitation? Do you think I got an invitation? Nobody got an invitation; what are you talking about? You just go! Don't worry! All the women of my family are going, everybody is very nice, the women will look after you, don't worry, don't worry."

I had never been to a *Rebbishe* wedding before, but I must admit that I was quite curious. I had only seen pictures and videos and wondered what it would be like to actually experience it. I don't belong to this particular group, and the fact that I did not get an invite really made it uncomfortable for me to just go. What if they send me away? What kind of gift would be appropriate to bring for the bride?

Challenges in being black and Jewish

I knew that if I went to this wedding, I would have many different sets of eyes all looking at me at once, watching my every move, scrutinizing me, and trying to figure out who and what I am, how religious and "authentic" I am based on how I look, what I wear, every move I make, even my body posture, and every word I say. I knew that women would openly, obviously, and shamelessly gossip about me while looking and pointing at me. I was and still am very capable of handling such pressure of constantly being stared at by many at once. Staring people cannot diminish my confidence.

It also happens often that a woman says something about me in Yiddish, especially about my skin color, and when I became a mother, about my children, wondering "why they are so white" and "if they are really mine." While I stand right in front of them, they would say something not so nice about me in Yiddish, thinking I don't understand anyway while I would understand every word. Depending on what they said, what they wondered about, I would answer them back in Yiddish to clarify their wondering. Then, while they were really obnoxious before, gossiping right in front of me, sometimes trying to ridicule me, they would then answer me back very friendly, explaining why they said what they said before as if their gossiping and remarks were justified in that way and not meant to be rude while really, it was super rude.

Hasidic men do not gossip as obvious as women do, but I do catch some here and there. Even though a man is not supposed to be looking, let alone staring at a woman, sometimes it seems like some Hasidic men just cannot believe their eyes when they see me or something and just stare me down as if they see something unbelievable, not from this planet.

Often, it happens as well that I am treated overly nice as if I am a *nebach* (an unfortunate person) and as if I need extreme kindness so it would perhaps "make me feel better" or something. I prefer and like it better when people just behave normal and natural towards me. In general, everybody treats me with kindness, so the assumption that I need special treatment because "the Jewish Hasidic world is probably mean to me because of my dark complexion" is really incorrect. I somewhat understand the staring, I probably would stare also.

I do realize and often think about the different ethnicities I consist of. Besides sprinkles of Irish, Portuguese, Middle-Eastern, German, and Scandinavian genes, my main ethnic makeup consists of Black, Jewish, and Chinese - seriously, the three ethnic groups who are and have been discriminated against, probably the most.

I am proud of who I am but sometimes laugh at the coincidence of this combination and wonder how and why the one upstairs made me who I am. I am made out of all these different ethnic groups who are often victims of discrimination, and these three groups often do not necessarily like and understand each other or get along either. It is not always easy, and I don't always have the patience to explain myself.

I do find it a privilege, in some crazy way, that the almighty entrusted my soul to go back to Earth and carry out the role as a black Jewish woman with some random Chinese genes as well and to just own myself as one and that wholeheartedly. He knows and trusts that I, the simple little me, can be this with pride and carry this out with pride. I have to do it, and I am proud. It just fascinates even me, even though I know that I am not the only one. There are more Hasidic Jews of color.

I know of this one family of color living in the same neighborhood as me. They were not Hasidic but clearly quite orthodox. On a regular basis, I was asked the question if I am related to that family. I would answer, "No, why?" while I knew very well why they would assume this.

"Oh no, you just look like the mother a little bit."

"Look like the mother, how? Are you related to the Katz's and Cohen's, and Goldman's? You look like them too," I would say then. This would end the conversation instantly. I did not look anything like the mother of that family except for that we have the same complexion. I was much taller, and my face was shaped way different.

I wonder if people ask that mother the same question as well, "Ooh! Are you related to Sara Braun? You look like her," really meaning, "She is black and Jewish like you."

I remember seeing an interview with a young black Hasidic teenager who lived in a Jewish Hasidic community in Brooklyn but in a different one from mine. Right next to his community, there was a large black community, and the two communities had a history of constantly disagreeing with each other to the point where it often turned to violence. The young man that was interviewed was asked all sorts of uncomfortable questions about being Jewish and black, really putting him on the spot. He was clearly careful about how he answered these questions, trying not to insult his community nor the black community "next door," as he could be considered part of both communities really. I often feel like I am in a similar boat. I root for black people just as much as for Jewish people.

When I walk in the streets outside of my Brooklyn community dressed modestly and perhaps a little old-fashioned, it happens way too often that other black ladies look at me as if they want to say "Look back at me the wrong way, and I'll beat the *** out of you." So I always automatically smile, and then they often smile back. I was called a "rich bitch" for no reason, and it is often assumed that I have a Caucasian husband. Even within my own family on my father's side, I sometimes feel like I have to humble down a little in order not to be perceived as arrogant because I did not choose to live their way but the Jewish way.

Once, I was at a family birthday party of the daughter of my father's brother. One of my cousins had a baby who must have been around five months, and I was holding the baby in my lap, talking to him, and playing with him. Sometimes, babies like to stretch and flex their leg muscles, especially when they are excited; they kick. This baby was doing that while smiling and flapping his arms, and I was encouraging this. One random aunt, who I really did not know personally, told me not to let the baby stand in my lap because his muscles were still too weak. The baby was not even standing in my lap; he was kicking his feet around while I held him up. She really did not say it in a nice way either, which immediately rubbed me the wrong way, and she said it the moment that the music stopped playing so everybody could hear her scolding me. She could have told me from the moment the baby was kicking while the music was still playing or more in private instead of hollering.

I explained that I am raising three sons who all used to be babies as well, and they are all happy and healthy boys. I know how to handle a baby, and thank you.

The first question I was asked after "Who do you think you are! You think you are better than us!" blablabla. I calmly asked, "Us who?" She had this presumption, only because I told her that I know how to hold a baby?

Back in the day when you sign up at a high school, they would ask you for your religion as well on the registration form, and they did their best to try to acknowledge, consider, and respect everybody's religion somehow in the values and morals of the school, so everyone knew that I was Jewish. I was severely discriminated against and not even realizing this at the time.

The black students were open to hanging out with me but would bully me as well with me being Jewish. I was always slightly and indirectly excluded; there was always this small wall as I was reminded constantly that I am not totally "like them," I am Jewish, and "Jews are boring and sad miserable Hebrew people," and on top of that, I rode my bike to school and I sing opera, which are two totally not such cool things to do. In my experience, most black people do not like opera music at all. I was rarely included in hanging out outside of school hours with them as well. I was just not the thrill; rather Jewish and boring as heck with a sense of humor they could not relate to. Their sense of humor was humiliating each other and then laugh about it. I never understood this. How is it funny to speak negative about someone or their family and hurt someone else's feelings? There is this show on MTV that reminded me a lot of this. In this show there are two teams rap-battling against each other by insulting each other. I could not understand how this was funny but was always amazed by their talent, how fast and precise they could come up with rhymes. That part was the joy and entertainment for me.

The students that practiced Islam, oh my goodness, they were even worse. They would never, not ever hang out with me, and they never saw me as "me Sara" an individual, they saw "the Jew." It was not like, "Oh, there goes Sara." It was, "Oh, there goes that Jew." My answers were "Jewish answers," my questions were "haha, dumb Jewish questions" my philosophy was not to be taken seriously or trusted because it came from a Jew unless it would help their grades. As if the ideas of the National Socialist party were still lingering around.

I was so used to this that it did not bother me, and I never even realized how disturbing this really was. My schoolmates did speak to me friendly and laughed with me, but I was constantly reminded that I was Jewish, and they would see me as a Jew first, while back then, being Jewish did not even mean anything to me. I was just Dutch first before I was Jewish, but in my mind, I was sometimes thinking, "What makes the 'Jewish me' different from other non-Jewish students?" We all shared the same interests.

I was listening to the same hottest music like everyone else, I wore jeans, and was always in for a good joke or prank. How would they feel about me if they did not know that I am Jewish? There were some grandchildren of ex-Nazis or Nazi sympathizers in my school as well; they would not speak to me at all, not even look my way. The neutral Caucasian Dutch students and the Asian students, mainly from India, did see "Sara" instead of "the Jew."

I, along with two other Jewish students, were the only Jews in school and we lived in a Jewish neighborhood in Amsterdam. These two girls were close friends of mine. One of them was Hanna. Hanna's father was not Jewish as well, and her mother was a typical Dutch Jewish lady with stereotypical dark hair, droopier eyes, and a larger hooked nose.

Hanna's parents were divorced, her father lived in a very busy neighborhood more toward the center of Amsterdam, and her mother lived in our neighborhood. Hanna lived with her father as she could not get along well with her mother and her mother's boyfriend at that time. She would visit her mother on a regular basis but would rarely sleep there.

Hanna had her own bedroom at her mother's apartment in the attic of the building. You could only reach Hanna's bedroom through the common stairwell, which was creepy to me because the neighbors had easy access to it as well at all times. Many older apartment buildings in Amsterdam have an attic where each family living in the building has a room to be used, mainly for storage. Many used it for storage, and others converted these rooms into extra bedrooms.

Hanna's mother often tried to convince Hanna to stay with her overnight but would absolutely not compromise her boyfriend for her daughter. I visited them a lot as well. Hanna's mother became very close to me, she would often cook what I liked to eat and always made sure to have cinnamon ice cream in the freezer as that was my favorite. I had a mother then, but Hanna's mother would also always be there if I needed anything.

This did not bother Hanna at all. She really could not care less. Hanna's grandmother used to be very active in the resistance group during the Second World War. Once she was on the Nazis' radar, she fled to Switzerland, where she stayed until after the war. Her grandmother loved to tell stories about the war. She was a strong and sharp lady. As old as she was, she could think and move fast, while Hanna's mother leaned more towards the opposite. She was a softer, naiver, and had a more sensitive soul, very peaceful, and just wanted to hang on to her boyfriend really bad.

Hanna could not connect to her mother's boyfriend very well and preferred to keep her distance from him. I witnessed how her mother always picked her boyfriend's side when there was an argument between Hanna and her mother's boyfriend. It seemed to me that it is probably his and her mother's submissiveness towards him that blocks Hanna from sleeping over there. Her boyfriend himself would not even sleep there most of the time. According to Hanna, he mainly lived at his "ex-wife's" house because he and his ex-wife shared a daughter, and he wanted to be there for his daughter. However, later he shared a baby boy with Hanna's mother as well but he still slept at his ex-wife's house. Hanna's mother believed and accepted his excuses.

During the graduation ceremony at my high school, when my name was announced to pick up my diploma from the principal on the stage, it was Hanna's mother who rushed to the stage to kiss and embrace me in front of everybody right after I received my diploma. Everybody started clapping and cheering, if you did not know me, you would think that she was my mother, while my own mother was sitting right there in the audience. My mother was absolutely livid. Hanna's mother did not even do this for her own daughter when she received her diploma from the principal. This left my mother with not such a positive impression of Hanna's mother.

Hanna's mother passed away suddenly in 2018. She was found unconscious by her teenage son on the kitchen floor. Since her mother passed away, Hanna won't speak to me, maybe because she assumes that I have a lot of questions about her mother's passing, which she is not ready or willing to discuss. Maybe I am wrong; I don't know.

My other Jewish friend from school, Marian Meijer, was exactly my height with super straight and very thick blonde hair. She was even more "boring" than me. Very quiet, with a shy little laughter, and did not say much creative or funny. She was a rational and intellectual thinker, just like both her parents. Every time I was at her house, her parents educated me a little more on my own history of South America, and that was their conversation with me, their way of socializing with me. They did tell me things I indeed did not know. It seemed like they only knew how to discuss history, research, and facts, never about what they liked or enjoyed, and why.

Marian did not show much passion or emotion towards anything either except for school and fencing. She dressed modestly, practically, and simple. She listened to classical music like myself, and played fencing professionally. None of my friends had this side to them, which she had, and I could relate to, to a certain extent.

The Rebbeshe Chasuna

(A wedding within a Rebbe's family)

It was difficult to decide what to wear to the wedding of the Rebbe's youngest daughter. There were a lot of extra rules pertaining to modesty, and I wanted to abide by them all. I ended up wearing a simple silk blouse with a long skirt down to my calves, thick black stockings underneath, and simple black high heels. I wore my hair in one long braid. I took the train to northeast Brooklyn, and after getting lost a few times in that neighborhood, I was eventually able to follow the sound of the music coming from the speakers of the wedding and walked right into a sea of mostly married Hasidic women, Bugaboo baby strollers, and girls of all ages who, in my experience, seemed to be dressed way too similar to each other, as if they all shopped at one certain store during a certain season, and at that one store only.

They had already gathered for the chuppah ceremony, and just as predicted, as soon as I was spotted and recognized as "another guest," I got stared at constantly. While being stared at and clearly gossiped about, I, too, was closely observing the whole scene and everybody I passed. If someone I passed was staring at me, I would say "mazel tov," and I got all sorts of different responses. Some would answer softly, "mazel tov," back while being stunned; others would answer "mazel tov" back loud, and cheery, being so pleasantly surprised. Some would not answer at all, just staring like they were thinking, "Huh? Did she just say 'mazel tov'?" Some would just nod, and I got all sorts of responses in between those. It seemed like everybody knew each other except for me.

Once everybody got sort of used to my presence, a small group of ladies approached me.

"*Mazel tov*!" They said with big welcoming smiles on their faces.

"What is your name?"

"Thank you, *mazel tov* to you. When is the *chuppah* starting? Do you know?" I answered.

The lady whispered in Yiddish to some of the other ladies she was with, asking what time the chuppah exactly started. They shrugged their shoulders a little and one answered back in Yiddish to just tell me that it would start soon.

"It will start any minute now... do you live in this neighborhood?" The lady asked.

"No, I do not..." I responded.

"Oh, so where do you live?" another lady asked.

"I live in Brooklyn as well, in another neighborhood." I purposely responded not wanting to immediately tell them where exactly in Brooklyn.

"Are you here by yourself? Do you know anyone here? What brings you to this *simcha* (celebration)? Uh,.. wedding?"

The lady assumed that I did not know what a "*simcha*" meant.

"Wow, so interesting, so where are you from?" one of them asked.

"I am from the Netherlands," I answered.

"Wow, really? Where is that exactly? That is Deutch, right? Not too far from Antwerpen? Oh wow," she said.

"No, it is Dutch. Deutch is German, and that's what they speak in Germany, Austria, and Switzerland; I am from Holland, and we speak Dutch," I corrected her.

Their first response to everything was constantly "Oh wow."

"Who are your parents? Are your parents from the Netherlands as well?" another woman asked.

"No, they are from South America," I answered.

Again, I had to hear, "wow, oh wow... they have Jewish schools in Holland? You went to a Jewish school?" This question was really a way of trying to figure out how long I had been Jewish, or if I was born Jewish at all, and then based on which school I went to, they would also know how religiously I was raised.

At this point, more women and girls had joined to listen and look at "this spectacle."

"No, I did not go to a Jewish school. I went to a very Dutch Christian school," I answered on purpose to cause more confusion. I did not want to give in to telling my whole story right away if they were not willing to ask me their questions straight up, so I pulled their legs a little.

"Do you have siblings? Where do they live? Where do your parents live now? What brought you here to New York?" they continued to ask.

At some point, one of the ladies finally had the guts to ask me, "You are Jewish, right?"

I smiled and answered in Yiddish, "If I am Jewish? What makes you wonder if I am Jewish? Are you Jewish?"

The ice was instantly broken with here and there some nervous laughs of relief. Arms got uncrossed, and shoulders relaxed, even children started to smile all of a sudden.

The questions continued in Yiddish,

"Wow! You speak Yiddish! Oh wow! Where did you learn Yiddish? How do you speak Yiddish?"

I would ask the exact same question back.

"Well, how do you speak Yiddish? I probably know it the same way you got to know it."

Some ladies left for a minute only to return with more women. Some actually asked me not to go anywhere. "I must meet their mother or sister or someone else, and they are getting that person right now."

It turned out to be a happy little gathering which started out tense. I immediately felt that the older generations, the *bubbes* (grandmothers), were in overall much warmer than the younger generations. They were really the ones that "looked out" for me, as Ari described.

They introduced me to everyone and praised me a lot. Every time I got introduced to someone, it was immediately mentioned in Yiddish that "she speaks a good Yiddish!"

During the *chuppah* ceremony, the ladies explained who was who under the chuppah making the different blessings, and everything that was going on, even though I already knew.

After the chuppah ceremony, it was not me wishing others "mazel tov" as I did when I first arrived. Now others came up to me wishing me "mazel tov."

One of the ladies I spoke with a lot throughout the evening invited me to come to her apartment. She had to feed her baby and put her baby and toddler in bed before the dancing at the wedding started.

"But I want to go to the wedding hall for when the bride and groom come out of the *yichud* room (a room where the bride and groom spend time by themselves after the *chuppah* ceremony)."

"Dancing won't start for a while; this is a Rebbeshe wedding *Sara'le*; everything takes so much longer! Haha!" Her name was Hindi Heller.

Short in height but a feisty lady with big icy blue eyes, a very pretty face framed in a short bob-shaped wig, and a hat on top of that. She was a bold lady who clearly took the initiative and charge.

She lived with her husband and about five young children in a small apartment in the middle of their neighborhood. Upon entering her apartment, I immediately stumbled upon one of her sons sleeping in a fold-out bed in the hallway.

The noise of us entering the apartment did not seem to interrupt him at all. In his clean pajamas, a large white head covering on his head from where you could only see his long side curls hanging out, under a fluffy white blanket, he was fast asleep. "There is not enough room in this tiny apartment for all of us," Hindi explained as to why her son was sleeping right next to the front door in her hallway.

I was a little bit surprised by this, but to Hindi, this was very normal, as if every household in her community had a child sleeping in the hallway. We talked about different topics while she was feeding her baby. Hindi spoke fast and had impressive analytical skills. She understood and saw through everything and ran her own little company while running a household with little children as well. She is a powerhouse.

We were talking about my background, my Jewish roots, and the different Hasidic dynasties, including the one she is part of. The one she is part of is split again into two groups run by two brothers who are both Rebbes. Each of the two groups is run separately by one of the two brothers, who are estranged from each other for various reasons. Hence, this particular Hasidic branch is split in two. The other brother established his community upstate in New York.

Hindi firmly suggested connecting to that community upstate, rather than the one in Brooklyn, to which her husband really belongs, but not her. Hindi was from upstate, and even though she preferred the community upstate for her own personal and political reasons, which I was not even aware of at the time, the differences she explained made me more curious about the community upstate. It sounded like it would perhaps be a better fit for me. According to Hindi, upstate, they are not so "*gashmiesdig*," which is materialistic, as they are in the city. It is more authentic, simple, and down-to-earth. That sounded just like the

Hasidic community in Antwerp to me, which is close to home.

"Don't stick to this, Rebbetzin; you should contact the wife of the other Rebbe from upstate. I will give you her contact information; she is wonderful, and you will love her," Hindi said.

Even though I was brought up modern and looked different from the members of this community, I immediately felt very natural and comfortable in this particular community. I don't even exactly understand why. But when I don't think about it and just be, then I understand.

I don't see myself living in this community as in many areas, it conflicts with my modern thinking and modernized lifestyle. However, it has become the absolute foundation of my life and that of my children also, in our own way.

We walked back to the wedding, which was now proceeding in a large wedding hall. I knew this particular hall and knew that it is usually split in two, one half used for the women and the other half for the men. Now, the entire hall was used for the women alone, as the Rebbe probably had most of the community attending his daughter's wedding. I noticed that there were many more women here than there were before during the *chuppah* ceremony. There was some light instrumental music playing while all the women were talking and laughing. I noticed many talking about and showing off their outfits or those of their daughters. When this happened, I too would take a better look at the outfit shown off and make my own opinions in my head about it, which was basically the same for each outfit: "Nothing special looks like what everyone else is wearing, and every Jewish clothing store is selling, but that's a cute bow she matched with it, or a nice belt she matched with it," or whatever.

There were no fresh flower arrangements or any other decorations but there was an overload of fruits and cakes being served. The staring and gossiping started all over again, and I went around again saying, "Mazel tov" to people. Some were laughing about it, especially the younger women who were in their late teens or early twenties or so and seemingly recently married themselves.

At some point, the music was turned up louder and accelerated. This was an indication that the bride was about to come out, so all the women started to gather by the large entrance door of the hall where they expected the bride to come out. I too, went over there but kept my distance a little bit. I was not used to such a wedding, especially not of this size, and I just wanted to observe the moment.

The bride came out. This super young skinny girl with a very pretty face, a delicate little smile looking like a doll, dressed in a wedding gown bigger than herself, and a turban-shaped white head covering made from tulle. She had her emotions and excitement under immense control and danced calmly with light, subtle arm, and leg movements being the perfect example of a beautiful, pure, modest Hasidic bride. The daughter of the big Rebbe. I had not experienced a bride so calm and collected yet. Usually, brides come out running into the hall with the biggest grin on their faces and jumping and dancing so enthusiastically that their veil almost falls off as well from time to time. There was nothing like this whatsoever at this wedding.

At some point, out of the blue, the *Rebbetzin*, (the mother of the bride) walked over to me from almost across the hall. You could see the other women's faces following her, wondering where she was going. She approached me with a warm smile, and her arms extended toward me. I understood that she wanted to dance with me, so I reached my arms back out to her. I noticed that this gesture of the *Rebbetzin* coming to me to dance validated my presence at this wedding. The women instantly showed support by holding hands, forming several layers of circles around us.

After a short moment, the bride was escorted to us as well to join the dancing. Her hands felt so cold, sweaty, and delicate. She seemed to be on autopilot. Maybe she was not, but that's how she appeared to me. I was wondering what was going on inside her head.

After all the dancing, we had to go to another place for the "*mitzvah tantz,*" literally "The mitzvah dance." This is a Hasidic custom where the bride stands still with one side of a gartel in her hands while a male family member(s) is holding the other side of the gartel while dancing. This custom usually only involves immediate family members of the bride and groom but not at this wedding. The whole community was invited to join and sit in for this part of the celebration as well, which was held in a makeshift stadium-like space.

Out of the four sides of the stadium, all the women were seated on bleachers on one side only, except for the bride and groom's immediate female family members. They were seated in proper chairs on ground level with their backs facing the rest of the women who were sitting on bleachers.

The entire side where all the women were sitting was covered from the men's view with a sheer foil curtain hanging from top to bottom for the sake of modesty.

It was very crowded on the bleachers and rather uncomfortable. We were sitting so close next to and on top of each other that I could smell the different scents of hair shampoo and laundry detergents from the women and girls all around me. There was a girl sitting in front of me; she must have been around twelve years old. She was so cramped that, somehow, she ended up sitting in between my legs with one of her elbows leaning on my knee and her head in her hand. Maybe she didn't feel well.

The foil curtain obstructed our view on some level, while the men could see everything clearly while singing and dancing. The bride looked like a little white fluffy snowflake in the middle of a sea of men all dressed in black. "She must be so exhausted," I was thinking.

I found the *mitzvah tantz* to be quite dreading as if it would never end, and I left in the middle of it all because I started to feel dizzy. It was too hot, too packed for me, and on top of that, very loud. The women noticed me all over again as soon as I got up, but this time, there were no funny looks. They all smiled politely and whispered "Mazel tov" while holding their right hand up and shaking it as if they were shaking another imaginary hand.

I walked down the bleachers, and the women and girls cleared the way with big smiles while saying "Mazel tov, mazel tov" and shaking my hand. This time, nobody stared at me with a big question mark written on their forehead. Nobody seemed to laugh at me or wonder about me "who is this dark lady?" It seemed like now everybody knew or was made aware of my presence and greeted me respectfully. That was nice.

This experience was so different from my daily life at that time. The feel and the energies were just completely different. It brought me back to something, but I cannot explain exactly what. As I sat behind my desk at work, my mind would often wander back to that evening. I did not necessarily feel like I was one of them, but I did recognize my self to a certain extend. My great-grandmother was Hasidic, and the Jewish spirit is something I genuinely feel in my core, in my heart. I cannot help this or change this. This is what it is. However, what I mean with "I do not feel like I am one of them" is that when I was at this *Rebbeshe* wedding, I did not necessarily feel like I was part of that Hasidic community, while when I saw a Hasidic woman, I do recognize myself. I am not talking about the color of my skin and the colors of their skin; it goes beyond that. Way beyond that, at the spirit, at the energy. I see myself. It is as if our spirits were created using the same mold. A "Jewish woman mold." There is nothing that anyone could do or say to change this. There is nothing that the holiest Hasidic woman or man could say to me that would make me believe or feel any less Jewish than he or she is. It's impossible.

Of course, I am more than just Jewish. This is obvious, and I recognize, honor, and acknowledge this. I treat everybody with the same level of respect, and I don't believe that the Jewish people are superior compared to other non-Jews either. I know for a fact that some of my non-Jewish family members have purer hearts than some of my Jewish family members.

It took me a while to fully process the night of the wedding. In my mind, I disassembled the entire evening and re-analyzed every little detail a few times: every facial expression, every smile, every insult, every remark, the music, laughter, body language, their way of speaking Yiddish, the makeup, which was for many women non-existent and on others way too obvious, but was supposed to appear "non-existent." I wondered about the Rebbetzin and what her life and that of her family must be like. She was treated like the queen of her community, and I wondered if she and her family lived somewhat like actual royalty as the royal families of Europe do.

I also wondered more about the men. I barely saw anything of the men and I was curious about them. What is their way of thinking? Is it like Ari's? How much do they know about the world around them outside of the community? What is their perspective on other Jewish men who are different from them? Are they narrow-minded like Devorah's father, perhaps? Or more open-minded like Yisroel, Aunt Chanshy's husband? Is it possible that there are a few that are worldly, like Joely, one of my closest friends? Joely is actually from that exact same community.

What about all those *shtreimels* (traditional high fur hats)? Are they comfortable to wear? They seemed heavy and uncomfortable to me. Do they ever fall off when they dance? Are they custom-made to fit their heads, so they stay on so well? I should ask Ari about this next time I speak to him. The most random questions, thoughts, and conclusions ran through my mind about that evening.

The lady, Hindi Heller, who I met that evening, called a few times as well to see how I was doing and just to schmooze. We spoke a lot about the community, which of course, made me think about the other community upstate. My head was in the more modern-Orthodox community, but my heart was in the Hasidic community. Even though my great-grandmother was not part of this specific Hasidic branch, I wanted to be more connected to this specific group and decided to reach out to the *Rebbetzin* Upstate. I wrote her a letter about myself, my background, and the reason why I was writing her. I wanted to be more connected but was not sure how to. I wrote the *Rebbetzin* from upstate New York, not expecting to hear anything back, at least not anytime soon, if ever. Such a person who is like a queen to thousands of people must be way too busy to read a letter from this random girl. Besides, she must receive so many letters and phone calls. Who am I to her?

But to my surprise, it did not take long before she actually called me. A kind lady spoke excellent English and had a clear voice like that of a newsreader. It was the *Rebbetzin* from upstate. When she called, I was at work and completely surprised to receive a phone call that fast and straight from *Rebbetzin* herself. I stepped out of my office to speak to her without any disturbances. Unlike others, she did not ask me the usual screening questions to see how and why I am Jewish. She was merely interested in my well-being and invited me to visit her at her apartment in Northeast Brooklyn. "Of course, I would love to." I responded. She informed me of the day and time she would be there and gave me her address.

I hung up, thinking, "Wow". As good as my intentions are, there are so many people out there with such heinous intentions, especially toward us Jews. Why did she blindly invite me like this? Perhaps someone from her niece's wedding informed her about me? However, I understood that her side of the family does not communicate with that side at all. What is it that made her invite me to her house like this?" I decided that she probably had security around her house, for her to be comfortable to invite a black stranger to her private house so easily.

I was invited on an early evening on a Thursday right before spring. I know it was on a Thursday because the following day would be the evening of Shabbat. I dressed exactly as how I like to dress, portraying who I am and what I am all about without any extra fuzz or false impressions. I arrived at her apartment, which was a beautiful ground-floor apartment in a typical Brooklyn brownstone building. There was no security around as far as I could see or notice, which I did not expect. She answered the buzzer herself and buzzed me in.

There in the doorway stood a simple, pious senior lady in modest Hasidic house attire and a turban. She was wearing glasses and had a strong, secure expression in her eyes, ready to face anything with poise and intellect. Her face reminded me of Eastern Europeans, Hungarians, to be exact. She radiated a nurturing nature and a lot of wisdom. She had a calm demeanor, soft, respectful, and she was kind, but very sharp. No nonsense. It looked like she could see right through anything. I sat across the dining table from her, where she seated me. She offered me a drink, which was poured into a beautiful crystal-like glass. I soon came to find out that 99.99% of the families in Hasidic communities have such glassware.

This time, I was asked a lot of questions about my background and my mother's lineage in particular. She found it fascinating like most people do, but she was not listening to me with the purpose of being amused like most, but rather to analyze it all and to figure out how to "place me" in her own mind.

She, in return, explained that she originally comes from the same *Hasidis* that my great-grandmother is from as well. The *Rebbetzin* of that *Hasidis* is her sister. "What a coincidence" I responded.

She also was very honest with me that it would be more difficult for me to get married within the community, because I am a person of color.

"I respect and accept you for who you are, but one person cannot change the whole City Hall," she explained.

"I know, and I have noticed how people don't instantly accept me or even take me seriously because I am black," I almost continued saying that this is based on their ignorance, but thankfully I filtered my words internally first before speaking them, and so I left that part out.

During our conversations, young men and teenage boys walked in and out for different reasons. They all called the *Rebbetzin* "mamie," but none of them actually were her biological sons she explained.

Some came to eat, some came to help with whatever, and she had a delivery as well for a huge, hot potato *kugel* which is a typical Jewish dish, mainly made out of shredded potatoes and eggs. It was delivered for Shabbat, which would be the following day.

Her house had such warm and pleasant energy about it. Very Yiddish and homey. It was also clear that she was surrounded by a lot of love from her people.

I spent about one hour with her, and in the end, she gave me the phone number of her very close friend Chana Goldstein, who is also the principal of the main girls' school of the community upstate. "She will be able to guide you very well," the *Rebbetzin* explained.

Going upstate for the first time

I left the *Rebbetzin's* apartment feeling even more positive about this community and wasted no time in calling Mrs. Chana Goldstein, who was as smart as a whip and super down to earth. Chana Goldstein had no problem telling anyone the ugly, dirty truth about anything in a classy and respectful way, and she had no patience for any type of nonsense or drama. She was absolutely fabulous, in my opinion. The mother of about ten children and who knows how many grandchildren and great-grandchildren, she invited me to her house upstate New York on a Sunday.

There is a Jewish bus company that drives a route from Brooklyn to upstate New York and back a few times a day. I was instructed to take this bus and to get off at a specific stop.

I got onto the bus and paid for the fare. A long, ugly checkered curtain ran through the middle of the bus from the front all the way to the end. This curtain served as a *mechitza*, a barrier between the men and the women, so the men would not get distracted by seeing and looking at the women. Sometimes when the bus stopped abruptly, the curtain would fly open halfway, and someone would get up in half a panic, closing the curtain again and, after a few times flying open, trying to secure it to the wall somehow or holding on to it. This is one of the things I just found to be so silly, especially because when men and women would get off or on the bus, the men and women brushed past each other, so closely you could clearly feel a man's arm, hip, or even his behind when he walks to his seat sideways. I am sure that they feel the body parts of the women as well.

Those narrow alleys in such charter buses are just as wide as one adult and are definitely not designed for two people walking next to each other. It often happens that men and women get on or off the bus at the same time, but because they can't see each other, they don't know how to avoid one another, and they brush right past each other, trying to get on or off. Perhaps this is all okay because one cannot see another? I never understood this.

It even happened to me while I was just sitting down in my seat, minding my business, a man was rubbing his butt onto the side of my shoulder and nearly my head because that man next to me on the other side of the curtain was putting away his stuff above his seat in one of those overhead storage spaces I think, maybe he was searching for something, I am not sure. He must have misestimated the space he had available behind him because the curtain was blocking that view of seeing how far exactly he could have stepped back and what exactly it was he would bump into when he did step back. I guess he thought that he was leaning against the side of a seat, but he was really leaning into me, rubbing his behind over my shoulder continuously. I literally put my hand on his *tuches* (butt) and slowly but steadily and firmly pushed it away from my shoulder and face. After two seconds of pushing, he realized what I was doing and quickly moved away. I purposely did it this way to make a statement.

It was a two-hour ride on the bus, and of course, I got off at the wrong stop because everything was just unclear and went too fast for me. I expected the bus to stop at actual bus stops with names displayed on them so I could see when I would arrive at my stop and get off. Since there was a curtain running through the bus, blocking my view from seeing the right side of the street, I could not see any bus stops or names. On top of that, I was also relying on the bus chauffeur to stop at every stop and announce the names of the stops. He did not stop at every stop and only announced part of the names of the stops. For example, if the name of a stop would be "Fischel Grunfeld Drive," he would just say monotonously "Greenveieild" through a crackling microphone with a thick Yiddish accent. Everybody else seemed to know exactly where they were and what stop to get off, except for me.

At some point, I walked over to the front of the bus towards the chauffeur and asked him when we would arrive at my stop. Without looking at me, he answered, "Hah?!" while keeping his mouth open, waiting for me to repeat my question. I asked again. "Aah!" He started to motion with his hand towards the back, "We passed this already, two! Two stops back already!" The bus was making so much noise while operating he had to scream. "Get off this next stop, and just walk down the hill."

I got off the bus and looked around me. There I was, standing. It was as if I had arrived in another country a few decades back. There were attached and detached houses with small, lush green grass fields in front of them, and here and there, a sign in Hebrew lettering in front of certain houses from people who run a business from home. Kids with the old-fashioned two braids in their hair or one simple short ponytail and in thick stockings, heavy knit skirts, and blouses, while all the boys had side curls and large black velvet head-coverings. They were all playing outside, riding bikes, playing jump rope, or just sitting around. Some mothers were in front of their houses as well, sitting on their porches or just standing at the door opening while watching their kids or talking to a neighbor.

As soon as I got off the bus, it was as if the world stood still. Every child stopped what they were doing, and all eyes were turned to me in no time. There I was, just standing there, taking everything in myself as well and not immediately realizing exactly which direction I should start heading into. Here and there, I saw more women, girls, and boys coming out of their houses or appearing in front of their windows to look at me. It was a beautiful day to be outside, and I got off at a busy stop in the middle of the afternoon when everybody was outside playing and enjoying the weather.

After a few seconds, I composed myself and just started walking down the hill, just as the bus chauffeur instructed me to do. I had no idea which street I was walking on or when to turn left or right or anything, but I acted as if I knew exactly where I was going. Here and there, a child would follow me on their scooter or bike to get my attention. I would just blink and smile; this would make the child smile back and stop following me or look surprised and stop following me. I just walked while carefully looking around me for any signs or street names.

When the bottom of the hill was approaching, I decided to ask someone how to get to this address, but the lady I asked had a hard time explaining this to me, seemingly not really knowing herself, and eventually, she asked me whose house I was going to.

"What! You're going to Chana Goldstein? Yah, yah, sure! She lives a few houses down."

The lady literally laid her hand on her heart when she said, "Chana Goldstein." I was really wondering why she was so surprised by this and now curious myself about this Chana Goldstein. She told one of her little kids in Yiddish to show me which house is the house of Mrs. Goldstein. The little girl instantly jumped up from the ground and ran way ahead of me towards a house in the far distance. At some point she pointed her finger at Goldstein's house. Mrs. Goldstein and her family were already standing outside to welcome me. "Sara! Welcome, welcome! How was your bus ride? Come in, come in. Really, don't be shy. These are just my daughters and some of their children."

Mrs. Goldstein had invited some of her children and their grandchildren as well to welcome and meet me. It was a loving but quite overwhelming feeling. Her daughters were very sweet and just grinned at me constantly, which made me shy. All the children were just staring. If a mother explained to them in Yiddish who and also what I was, the stare would be joined by another grin.

I was seated on a very comfortable brown soft leather sofa, which was against the wall, right beside the big dining table. Everybody was sitting around me, and I definitely felt like the center of attention.

In Holland, when you visit somebody, or someone visits you, you hang out in the living room. Usually, the living room has a designated area where the dinner table and chairs are, but that only takes a small part of the living room away. In Mrs. Goldstein's house, the dinner table was grand, clearly the most important piece of furniture. It was placed right in the center of her "living room," and her sofa was tucked away in a corner. On the other side of the dinner table stood a wide and tall China cabinet, often called a breakfront. It was full of silver.

I found myself getting comfortable pretty fast. Mrs. Goldstein is a very respected woman in this particular community. She is the principal of their girl's school, and every single woman, and probably men as well, know her. I expected a stiffer person who would come across as cooler, more held-back, and perhaps slightly arrogant. Mrs. Goldstein was not like that at all. She was actually super normal, funny, warm, and open.

Of course, I had to explain myself and my background again as to why and how I am Jewish, who else in my family is religious, and what Holland is like in terms of anti-Semitism, etcetera. But she was different from what I expected. I learned later that in the girl's school where she is the principal, she is not considered to be such a lovey-dovey person. I had women who walked me to her house, and as soon as we arrived, the tone in their voices would all of a sudden be so soft and respectful. I had girls walking me to her house, not even comfortable bringing me all the way to her door.

She explained that she knows a family in the community who will "take me under their wing." They would be a great *shidduch* for me, a great match. Their name is Mr. and Mrs. Farber, and they have sixteen married children plus two more adopted children. I was to become the third "adopted" daughter. Mr. and Mrs. Farber happened to live exactly across the street from where I mistakenly got off the bus earlier. I just loved this community and everything about it. Everything was just about family, community, good food, and creating beautiful memories with God at the center.

I couldn't help but wonder, though, why Mrs. Goldstein, with half her offspring and even the *Rebbetzin*, let me in so easily like this. And not just in their community but in their personal space. Especially me, a "*schwartzer*," a black person. Unfortunately, many Hasidim have this biased idea that black people are lazy drunks, that crimes are committed mainly by black and Hispanic people, that they cannot trust a black person, and they are sometimes even scared of black people. I could have been a complete maniac, and then what? Would they just let anyone in? What is it that made them welcome me like this? Maybe because I am from Europe? "Did they see the Jewish spirit behind the color of my skin?" I was thinking sarcastically. So many crazy things happen around us, which would make a Jew extra cautious, but nobody ever showed any discomfort or ever seemed to have doubts about bringing me around, on the contrary, I got absorbed and involved in everything.

There was one specific incident that nearly made me fall off my chair. This was when Mrs. Goldstein's youngest daughter was getting married. The sweetest girl, her name was Raize'le. Mrs. Goldstein brought Raize'le to my apartment to try on wedding dresses. While Mrs. Goldstein was concerned with how modest and tight a dress would fit, Raize'le was concerned about me, that I should not get insulted by her mother turning down too many dresses at once, and told her mother in Yiddish to let me work on her while knowing very well that most dresses were not an option for her.

On her wedding day, I sat at the table with Raize'le sisters and sisters-in-law. Her oldest sister Shevy was sitting next to me, and we were chatting about all sorts of things in English. Soon after that, I got into a conversation with another sister but this time in Yiddish.

Shevy responded, "Oh! I thought that you were more comfortable speaking English; I did not know you spoke Yiddish that well! And I am breaking my teeth trying to conversate in English with you, haha!"

We continued speaking in Yiddish, and while I was talking to her, she suddenly says, "You are black, but you really are a stunning lady, you know?"

I was completely shocked and responded with, "huh? What is that supposed to mean?"

She said, "Nothing special; I just don't think you would be accepted so much if you weren't so beautiful."

I could not help but just stare at her in disbelief. She quickly stroked me over my back with a smile and said "don't worry, I meant it as a compliment" and med into a conversation between two of her sisters sitting across the table about a completely different topic.

I was still sitting there, completely flabbergasted. "What did she just say? Did she actually just say that? Does she really believe this? And what does beauty have to do with this? Is it true what she says?"

Beauty is not something that you're supposed to openly look at or consider in the community. God won't judge you based on how beautiful, skinny, or how tall you are. Rather, God judges you based on the good deeds you do. If a boy or girl is not conventionally attractive but is from an exceptional family, you will still marry him or her, regardless of their looks. This is the idea. However, now I hear that the community accepts me because I am pretty, and if I were not, I would not have been accepted because I am black.

This idea stuck with me for a very long time, especially when meeting new people who would say, "You're so gorgeous, by the way!" I would immediately wonder, "Is that why you like me?" Later in life, I was blessed with handsome sons as well, and the beauty of my family became more highlighted. Thus, Shevy's statement had a negative effect on me, making me think negatively about people finding me beautiful first, I would wonder how genuine their kindness was.

The community in Manhattan and other communities alike became too "mild" for me. For Shabbat and Jewish holidays, I wanted and needed the full, heavy, and extra lengthy *heimishe chasidishe* (Hasidic) experience. There was no other option. I needed to live and feel it thoroughly. It got so bad that I would even judge other more modern families for not preparing or celebrating the way we did it. It was not good enough, in my opinion.

Especially for the holiday of Passover, I would cringe when I learned how "inaccurate" or "insufficient" some women would clean their houses or prepare their meals. What are they thinking eating *challah* bread in their dining room the Shabbat before Passover? This while the dining room has been completely cleaned for Passover already? Are you crazy? You are supposed to eat that in the kitchen, or better yet, on your balcony! Don't bring "*chametz*" (food with leavening agents) in your dining room! The fact that Sephardic Jews ate beans and lava bread on Passover was just beyond my comprehension or something. I became too radical.

I also got annoyed at work over how the kosher kitchens were taken care of. Besides the hygiene part, in my opinion, it was handled with too much disregard to *kashruth* (regulations of a kosher diet). When I used to see one of the Hispanic maintenance guys that worked for the Synagogue that resided in the same building jokingly slamming his ham and cheese sandwich on the kitchen counter, I would think, "what an idiot." But now, I would have had him fired. You are not even supposed to bring that "*treyfah*" (non-kosher) sandwich into the building, let alone in the kitchen! Let alone slamming it onto the counter on purpose!

Sometimes on Fridays, I did not have enough time after work to get groceries at my local grocery store for Shabbat. I would then go to a very expensive kosher supermarket in Manhattan. Their ready-made Shabbat dishes were not befitting to me. Especially their potato kugel. It had to be "*heimish*" (from/like home) for me for it to be a proper Shabbat potato kugel. The size of their potato shreds was just way too coarse for it to be considered a *heimisha* kugel. The chicken soup is wrong too. Why does the broth have small pieces in it? I was thinking. It is supposed to be a clean and clear soup with whole cleaned carrots, large chunks of zucchini, and maybe a "*kneidl*" (a matza ball) but not like this. What is this?

I became pretty extreme, too extreme if you would ask me now. I started to feel more and more out of place at work in Manhattan as well. *Yiddishkeit* (the Jewish way of life) was too much "watered down" for me there. I often went upstate for Shabbat to Mr. and Mrs. Farber's house.

The first time I was invited for Shabbat to Mr. and Mrs. Farber's house, I packed my little bag and took the bus upstate again. This time I acted as if I take this bus all the time. I told the bus driver in Yiddish that I wanted a round-trip ticket for one person and laid out the exact cash. I could not give it to him directly in his hand, as Hasidic men don't take small items from women's hands to avoid accidental touching. So, I put down the money for him. When the bus arrived in the "*shtetl*," (A small Jewish village) I started to focus like an eagle and knew exactly where to get off. My suitcase was kept on the bottom of the bus and was pushed all the way to the back by the suitcases of other passengers who got onto the bus after me. This young and silly me had no problem crawling halfway into the cargo hold of the bus to grab my suitcase.

Mr. and Mrs. Farber lived right across the street from the bus stop, so it did not take long for me to find their house. It was a beautiful sunny day, and I was standing in front of their duplex, bracing myself before going up the steep concrete stairs that led up to their front door. I knocked on the door, but nobody opened up. I was thinking, "Maybe this is not their front door but a door to a shared hallway where there are more front doors?" From the outside, it was hard to see how many apartments there were in this duplex and where one ended and the other one began. I had no idea. I just opened the door and realized that I had stepped right into their house. In the long hallway I stepped into, I was met with a mixture of smells of potato kugel, cholent (a stew of beans, meat and potatoes), and fresh laundry. I will not ever forget this combination of scents. It was the first thing that welcomed me at my first Shabbat in the community, where I found my other family, the community that left such a positive and profound impression on me. I left my suitcase in the hallway and walked towards the next door I saw in the near distance.

I opened the door, and there stood Etty. She noticed me right away and smiled at me while walking towards me with open arms. "Welcome, welcome! So nice that you came, such a prestigious guest we have!" she said in Yiddish while hugging me. Her older sister Leah was sitting on the sofa and approached me as well in the meantime. Leah was not as warm as her younger sister, but she politely greeted me while shaking my hand. In the meantime, Etty was screaming, "Mamie! Mamie! Ze is du!" which means

"Mamie, she is here!" Two seconds later, there stood an older, short lady with glasses on and a turban on her head. This is Mamie Farber, a typical Hasidic lady, exactly how one would imagine a Hasidic lady to be. She walked over to me, also with her arms wide open, and kissed me on my cheeks.

With a heavy accent, she said, "Welcome; I am so happy you came. Please feel at home. Sit, sit. I will get a piece of kugel and seltzer. How was the ride on the bus?" There were quite a few children as well. I was introduced to every single one of them, but to me, they all looked alike, and I could not tell them apart that quickly, let alone remember their names. Leah immediately explained to me that her husband is the younger brother of her father. So, her husband is her uncle as well. Even though I am aware that this often happens within this community, I was quite shocked to hear this, especially the tone in how this news was related to me, so calm, so normal, like "everyone marries their uncle all the time" or something.

I actually became very close to Leah's oldest daughter, Chaya-Hindi. We could talk on the phone for hours. Chaya-Hindi was very curious about the outside world and Europe and often had questions. In the spring and summer, we would sit on Mamie Farber's porch for hours, just talking about everything and nothing. Many family members, other children, and grandchildren of Mamie Farber came and left throughout the day, and I got to meet many. Mamie Farber also has one son who decided to take a few steps back from being a full-blown Hasidic man.

He had no side curls and lived a more modern life. Also, his wife wore a wig instead of a silk headscarf, and more form-fitting clothing, while all his sisters are much stricter and wear silk headscarves and much more loose-fitting clothing. This brother's name is Moishe. He came in, looked me in the eyes, and just greeted me, while none of his brothers and brothers-in-law would look me in the eyes at any given moment. He tried to come across like he was the "cool" one by making a lot of jokes and talking about things Hasidic men mostly don't know or would not talk about. He was also making smart or actually derogatory remarks towards his sisters.

One of his sisters had just had a baby, and this was the first time he had met the baby. Babies are born so often in this family that it is nothing very special. His sister had dark brown hair before she got married and shaved it off, and dark eyes. All her children had dark hair and dark eyes except for her new baby. He quickly glanced at the sleeping baby in the stroller and said to his sister in English, so I could understand and perhaps laugh, "She is blonde! Who is her father?" then he glanced at me with a smile on his face.

But I couldn't laugh. I was rather confused and surprised by his boldness. His sister was super embarrassed and answered back in English, "What do you mean? You know who the father is." And out he was again on his way.

Mamie Farber's husband, Tate Farber, was a very pious man with very thick glasses and long white/gray side-locks, eyelashes, brows, and a beard. He had a slight bend in his back when standing and walking.

Tate Farber clearly did not care about anything materialistic at all. He serves God. That's what is important, and that is absolutely it. He is a huge Jewish scholar as well and has always worked within the Rabbinical circle. Tate Farber also would in no way look me in the eyes. However, he did make an effort to speak to me and make me feel comfortable and at home. I was absorbed in the family, and it did not take long before I had to fetch my own drinks from the kitchen and help out with setting and cleaning off the table.

Soon I was considered and treated like another Farber sister, even the younger children believed that I was another actual "*mieme*," which means aunt. I would treat the kids exactly how I would treat my sister and brother's kids as well. One Shabbat afternoon, I was reading in my bed while all the adults went to lie down for a nap. Most of the kids were playing while one or two of the teenagers were watching them. At some point, I fell asleep as well. About an hour and a half later, I woke up with two kids, Etty's twin daughter and son snuggling up against my back, sleeping in their beautiful Shabbat clothing. It was the cutest thing. I could not believe that I did not wake up by them getting into my bed. Today these two kids are teenagers, and I am not allowed to pinch the boy's cheeks anymore.

The haircut ceremony of my second son Moishe at the house of mamie and tate Farber.

Me with two of my children at a Farber wedding

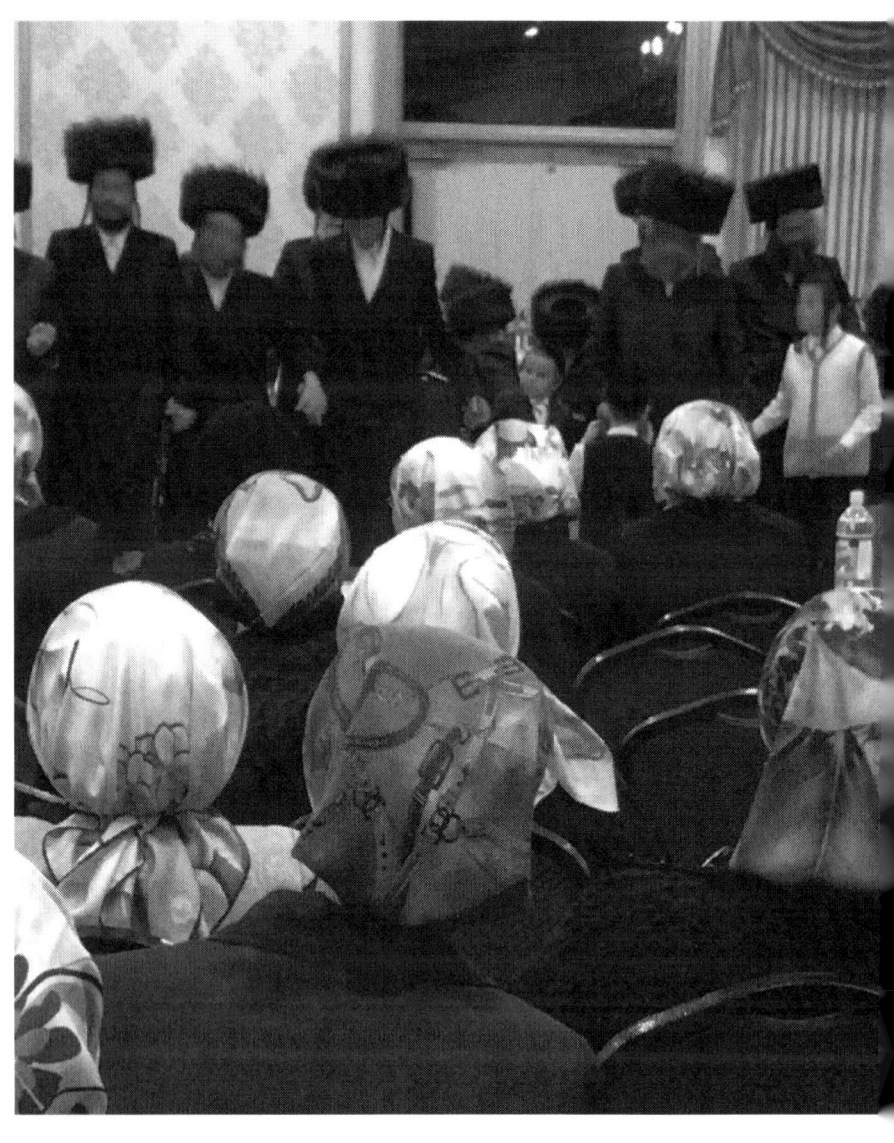

My youngest son Meijer during the *mitzvah tantz* at the wedding of a Farber grandchild.

Ski trip to Vermont

At work in Manhattan, we were putting together a fun ski trip for our young members in Vermont. It was something we did every winter, and it was always a lot of fun to organize with my co-workers. The plan was for me to stay behind with Rabbi Weis's personal assistant to take care of the office while everybody went away on the ski trip.

On the day of the trip, I took care of the last-minute administrative logistics in the office. It was Thursday, and the big charter bus would leave with the staff and the group in the evening. The bus was rented from the same bus company that always takes me upstate to the Farbers. The bus was operated by one of their own drivers as well, and the bus driver happened to be the eldest brother of one of our participants who was looking to leave his Hasidic community. His name was Fishl when I met him, but he later changed his name to John. He used to come around at our events still with his side locks, but he no longer had these when we went on our ski trip.

I was notified by the maintenance staff of the building that our bus had arrived and stood in front of the building. I went downstairs to inspect the bus, making sure everything was ready to go and to communicate to the driver times and logistics. The big bus was standing right in front of the building where the Jewish Ambulance usually parks. The bus was open with the motor running, but the bus driver was not on the bus. I took the initiative to go into the bus anyway to check. All seemed fine, and just as I was about to step out of the bus, a young, tall, skinny, very handsome Hasidic man jumped on and stood still on the first step, looking right into my eyes.

There was an awkward silence as we stared at each other, so I broke the silence by saying,

'I'm sorry, I thought you were Fishl.'"

"No, I am his brother. What is your name?" he replied.

I felt a little stupid saying that, even though you could clearly tell that Fishl was related to this bus driver who was his brother. Fishl was so much shorter, almost a whole foot shorter.

Fishl's brother was truly a handsome man, something I do not necessarily find in general about Hasidic men. He was very masculine, with the sleeves of his white shirt rolled up to his elbows, comfortable black shoes on, and his side curls done in the morning and not so perfect anymore. He was a fast mover and comfortable in his skin; he did not seem so stiff, mortified about the unfamiliar and slow. He seemed quick, confident, and aware. He had striking blue eyes, very dark hair, and a dark beard. I immediately noticed and liked this contrast. He had a little bit of a sloping forehead as well, which placed his eyes more in a shadow below his forehead. Because of this, the color of his eyes would jump out even more. Really stunning.

We could get along from the get-go, and there was an instant connection and friendship. Instead of me going back upstairs to my desk right away, I ended up hanging out with Fishl's brother on the bus for a little bit, just talking about everything and anything. His name was Shmuel. I feel like I got to know him really well in the short time that we were talking. He was smart, funny, and just a lot of fun.

I got off the bus, and Shmuel followed me off. Before I went onto the elevator, we got into conversating again. One of my co-workers interrupted us at some point by saying, 'I am sorry to break up this *shidduch*, but we have to go.' (A shidduch is a match, usually between a man and a woman) It was already dark outside, and our ski participants slowly started to arrive one by one.

I got back to my office. Before the bus left for Vermont, Shmuel asked me for my phone number. He lives Upstate as well, in the same community as Mrs. Goldstein and Mamie Farber. He has a wife and six children, and he would like to invite me for Shabbat one time. We exchanged numbers, the bus left, and I went home exhausted.

When I got home, I was debating if I should prepare for Shabbat tonight or tomorrow after work. I was so exhausted but was afraid I would not have enough time to do everything at once the following day before sundown. I decided to do the cooking and cleaning of my large kitchen that evening, and I would put the sheets in the washing machine in the morning before leaving for work. Then I would finish up my living room while my bedding is drying after I get back from work early in the afternoon the following day.

I started cooking right away and was making a potato kugel when I received a text message from Shmuel. He asked how I was doing, that it was really nice meeting me, and that they were cruising along beautifully on the bus. I responded friendly, telling him that I was doing great. Nice meeting him too, and I asked why he was texting while driving. I also mentioned that I was exhausted but in the middle of making a potato kugel. He flattered me by telling me that he would love to taste a piece of my potato kugel.

"Well, that would be hard while you are in Vermont, but maybe they will serve kugel tomorrow night over there," I responded.

He asked me why I won't come up there with my kugel to join them for the weekend. I couldn't go to Vermont because someone had to stay behind at the office, especially for the ski participants that leave from the city tomorrow instead of tonight.

Ironically enough, I got a phone call from Rabbi Weiss shortly after, asking me if I could please come up to Vermont the following day and bring his luggage along, which he had forgotten at his apartment. My first thought was, "How is it possible that you on a trip, and forget your luggage?" I could not understand. I told Shmuel about this. "Wow! This is more than a coincidence! You were meant to be here with me! Come up here and join us! You can take my car."

Shmuel had his car parked at the bus base of the company we rented the bus from in North-East Brooklyn. For some reason, he had left his keys in his car as well, hidden right behind the little door of his gasoline tank opening. "Why did he leave his car keys behind?" I was wondering and asked him later in a text message. "Because I knew you would need it to be with me in Vermont," he answered. He was very flirtatious, but I have met a lot of flirtatious men and did not think much of it. I had no GPS, and Shmuel explained precisely how to get up there, which highways to take, which exits to get off etcetera. It was a two- and a half-hour drive, and it seemed like it would never end. I was listening to the music of a famous festive Hasidic singer in his car. Now, every time I listen to that same music, I think of Shmuel and snow and relive the car ride to Vermont.

Shmuel called me at some point to see if everything went well. I told him as a joke that I was completely lost and had no idea how to continue. The poor guy tried to locate where I was and figure out how to get me to the resort until I told him that I was joking and should be there shortly. "Ooh!" he said. "I was thinking you must be really stupid to get lost," he told me boldly. I was laughing, loving this bold remark this Hasidic guy just dared to throw at me.

The closer I got to the resort in Vermont, the more mountains and snow I saw around me. It was beautiful. I arrived about an hour before sunset and had to hurry up to get ready. First, I had to get Rabbi Weiss's suitcase to him. I went to his room or suite, and he opened the door with merely a towel around his waist, grabbed his suitcase, thanked me friendly, and quickly closed the door. Not because he was embarrassed but because he was in a rush to get ready before sundown.

There was no room assigned to me yet, so I got myself ready in one of my friend's rooms, who was a participant. I wore a silky black dress with black patent leather heels. My hair was halfway up as always, and I curled it with a curling iron. I went downstairs to check the premises and the kitchen, and as I was walking, I again bumped into Shmuel unexpectedly as he all of a sudden came flying from around the corner. No one else was around. Shmuel was very happy to see me, I could see it in his eyes. He said, "You look so beautiful!" while holding his arms and hands open and up. I was not sure if he expected a hug or if this was just his body language expressing how beautiful I looked. "Thank you. You look beautiful too," I answered back rather sarcastically.

He was wearing his *shtreimel* and *beketshe*, which are traditional Hasidic garbs to wear on Shabbat, holidays, or family celebrations like weddings, etcetera. His *shtreimel*, which is a large round fur hat, was set on his head a little crooked as if he were some sort of a gangster. I loved it. He was not your ordinary Hasidic guy; Shmuel was not boring and just full of life and swag.

The Shabbat dinner was a lot of fun. There were about eight round tables set up with ten people per table. I was not sitting at Shmuel's table but with the rest of my co-workers. We laughed a lot, sang a lot, and clapped our hands a lot to the singing. You could hear Shmuel's singing and clapping above everyone else's.

Towards the end of the dinner, some of my co-workers and I started to walk around and have small chats with each table, making sure everyone was comfortable and having a great time. When I approached Shmuel's table, he had his back turned towards me, but somehow, he knew I was approaching his table. While someone was talking to him, and I only saw the back of his head, he extended his arm towards me and motioned with his finger to come to him. Once I was standing behind him, he motioned to the empty chair next to him to sit down. It was as if he had eyes in the back of his head, and I was blown away by this. I sat down, and he put his arm around me for a quick two seconds, acknowledging my presence, and then continued listening to the guy who was talking to him.

I patiently waited for him to finish his conversation while trying to figure out how he knew I was approaching his table. Once the guy finished talking, Shmuel again put his arm around my shoulders again, pulled me against him, kissed me on my head, and said to the guy, "Isn't this woman beautiful?" The guy and I were both taken by surprise. The guy answered, "... yes.... she totally is," with an awkward smile on his face. I think Shmuel had already drunk too much and loosened up a little too much.

A few hours later, after half the people had gone to bed or hung out in the lounge room of the resort, Shmuel and I separated ourselves from the rest in the sauna area and continued to talk. Nothing inappropriate happened; we just talked a lot. He wanted to learn a lot about me, and I was curious about him. We also talked about Hasidic women, and to my surprise, he did not find anything attractive about a Hasidic woman. He was making fun of the women from his community, especially of the hats the women in his community wear. "As if they just drop it on top of their heads without actually putting it on." He was motioning how a woman would hold a hat above her head with extended arms and then just let go of it.

Only later did I come to realize that he was indirectly talking about his own wife. Everything he disliked about a Hasidic woman is exactly what his own wife embodied. I told him that I had just met Mrs. Goldstein, who lives in the same community upstate as him. At that time, I had not met Mamie Farber yet and was not yet as engulfed in the ways of living the Hasidic lifestyle. I was much freer and more accepting. Shmuel knew Mrs. Goldstein as well; he found her to be one of the cleverest women he knew, and he just could not believe that I had been upstate to his community. He tried to test me by asking what the color of the roofs was there. Who would remember or even pay attention to that? He was drunk, however, and was very comfortable putting his arms around my shoulders constantly. I think he really longed for a connection and affection.

The following day he seemed a little embarrassed about how he had behaved the evening before. Of course, a Hasidic man is not supposed to look at, and definitely not touch, any woman besides his own wife.

Shmuel and I ice-skating in Vermont.

I wanted to leave my job, but I was not in the financial position to quit. I started to design, produce, and sell modest wedding gowns on the side of my apartment. Beautiful gowns with long sleeves and high necklines. I really enjoyed this. My kitchen was large and situated right by the front door of my apartment. Every Sunday, my kitchen would turn into a gown boutique. I would close off part of my kitchen with a curtain where the kitchen counter and fridge were standing. The curtain was specially placed in this position to split my kitchen in two.

I advertised in local papers and magazines and got customers from all over the city and from all levels of observance, from brides that wore pants during the week and skirts on Shabbat and didn't have any plans on covering their hair in any way after they were married to brides from strict Hasidic backgrounds, that wore skirts no shorter than six inches below their knees with the thickest pantyhose under those skirts and who will shave their heads once they are married. It was quite interesting to me. There were specific habits and personalities that went with it, and I constantly had to adjust myself. There were certain things I could say to a Manhattan bride that I absolutely could not say to a Hasidic bride. The same went for making suggestions. I knew the limits quite well, having worked in Manhattan, spent a lot of time upstate New York, and lived in Brooklyn. I constantly learned something new about the different lifestyles, especially upstate. Whenever I was there, if there was anything that was different from how I knew it or unfamiliar to me altogether, it was explained to me right away. So much so that at some point, I felt like I could be a proper Hasidic wife myself once I got married.

Most of my customers were Hasidic customers from Brooklyn, and I noticed that the more religious a mother and bride were, the pickier they were in choosing and actually buying a gown. Brides from Manhattan were the easiest and just a breeze to sell a gown to. They were always super friendly and stress-free, picked what they liked, paid full price for it up front and never complained or asked for a discount. Manhattan brides made no more than two appointments for fittings, and off they went without any fuss. Alterations on a gown of a Hasidic bride were a whole other story. It did not matter how much you thought the gown fits perfectly and was done; the bride, her mother, or one of her sisters would always find the smallest or silliest thing that was not good enough and needed some more or less of something or some sort of fixing, increase, decreasing, or whatever.

At some point, I felt like it was not worth so much of my time anymore, and I would mainly want to focus on Manhattan brides until I found that this was not something I wanted to do for the rest of my life. I slowly stopped as I lost interest and patience.

Me dressing up a bride.

180

My wedding

I got back in contact with a girl I grew up with in good old Holland. From when I was seven, we would play with each other almost every day and sleep over at each other's house often as well. Her name was Inge, she was two years older than me, and she used to have a crush on my oldest brother.

Inge had vicious ways about her. She always had to control absolutely anything and everything. Her own mother was scared of her, and her younger brother Manfred. They would sometimes completely terrorize their mother. That household was completely out of control, as there was nothing that their mother could tell them to do. If they did not want to do it, they simply would not, and their mother would have no legs to stand on. It was so crazy that Inge was even able to groom her mother to bring a cold drink to her bedroom every time Inge banged on her bedroom wall.

She had every cool toy a little girl like myself could have wished for because her mom, who was on welfare, would buy anything Inge wanted, even when she really did not have the money. They would just force their mother to buy whatever they wanted at that moment anyway. I think that it was more the toys that appealed to me rather than a friendship with Inge herself. She just had the coolest toys. Her mother gave me a lot of affection and attention as well. She liked me and always found me really cute. She laughed softly in enjoyment over almost everything that came out of my mouth and was immediately alarmed by any little "booboo" I had. My mom definitely did not do that. Inge's mother would jump up to prepare a hot meal if I was a little hungry and would jump up to get a drink for me when I was somewhat thirsty. I was also allowed to move around her house as if it were mine and had unrestricted access to every space.

Despite all this and all I witnessed, I was never disrespectful to Inge's mother and showed appreciation for everything she offered me and did for me. I think that her mother craved and liked that as well. I do not think that my mother would have allowed me to play over at Inge's house if she had been aware of how rebellious Inge and her brother really were and how their mother would give in the way she did. My mother was nothing like Inge's mother. There was no way I could be disrespectful to my mother in any way, shape, or form at all, not ever. If I said to my mother that I was thirsty, she would probably have said "*mazel tov*" or something. Not even trying to relate it to the fact that I wanted her to get a drink for me from the kitchen while knowing exactly that it is a drink what I would want from her. She would always make tea for me because I was not allowed to handle boiled water by myself, and maybe, if she was in the kitchen already, she would bring a drink for me, but that was as far as it got.

I was taught to take care of myself and the animals we had from a pretty young age. I even made my own scrambled eggs at the age of eight without direct supervision. I baked cookies and cakes as well at that age. Inge certainly was able to do many things for herself; she just did not want to. Her bedroom was so full of stuff, that there was no room to walk on the actual floor. You would have to walk over her toys.

Inge had a brother named Jacques-Laurent, who was older than her and was born in a small village in North-West

France. Unlike his siblings, Jacques-Laurent had a different biological father and looked very different from them. Inge and her younger brother Manfred had dark straight hair, dark eyes, and slim builds, which matched their slim, tall dark father's appearance. In contrast, Jacques-Laurent had reddish-blonde hair, light-colored eyes, and a broad, muscular build like his mother's family. He had a square jawline and was often mistaken for being Russian. Jacques-Laurent's mother gave birth to him at a young age in a time when children born out of wedlock were not accepted, and he never met his biological father until he was a teenager. These life instances had an impact on him, shaping how he viewed himself, the world, and who he became as a man, husband, and father.

When I was in my early twenties, I spoke with Jacques-Laurent more and more frequently. He was kind, patient, and could be sarcastic and silly like me. The fact that I had known him almost all my life made our friendship extra comfortable and trusting. We could speak about anything for hours at a time, from big musical artists to the foods we ate, to different cultures and history. It was very clear that he preferred women of color to Caucasian women, finding Caucasian women boring-looking and "nothing to it," as he explained. Even though he was Jewish, he personally did not care if a woman was Jewish or not. Jacques was single and had a young son with his ex-girlfriend, who was also a woman of color. His little boy's name ironically was Noam.

To my surprise, Jacques revealed that Noam was living with a foster family. Jacques explained that Noam's mother was not in the right state of mind, smoked a lot of marijuana, and had poor judgment when it came to raising her son and making appropriate decisions for him. Psychologically, she was also not doing well. This was, of course, according to Jacques; I did not know her personally.

"Why isn't Noam living with you?" I asked. "Are you not well either?"

Jacques laughed as if I had made a joke, but I was dead-serious, quite confused, and surprised that a parent would let their child live with strangers when they were available to be a parent themselves. Jacques explained that Noam was living with his foster family, together with his older half-brother, who his mother had with another man.

"It's better for them to be together, and besides, I work every day," Jacques said.

I still could not comprehend his reasoning for why he couldn't take his own son in.

"The fact that you work really should not be the deal-breaker as to whether your child lives with you or not. Most parents work and raise children, Jacques. And if it is so important that he is together with his half-brother, more important than being with his own father, why won't you just take them both in then?"

Realizing how much of a big deal this was to me, Jacques now blamed it on the social workers, saying that it was their decision that Noam should live with a foster family instead of with his father. I was thinking "the simplicity of it all." Jacques talked about it so lightly, as if it did not matter much, as if he was talking about the child of some dude he read about in a magazine, completely unrelated to him, as if he was completely unbothered by the situation.

This conversation with Jacques was the first time I realized how my ideas of what it means to be a parent and how much I value this differs tremendously from his. Jacques's father was never a parent to him until Jacques was 16, so now it seems like he unconsciously thinks that it's okay not to be a parent to his little boy and devote himself to his child. Although Jacques believes he's a wonderful father this way, I find it unacceptable. There would not be one day in my life that I would not fight for my children, and if a social worker were to decide that they were better off with strangers, I would not be able to talk about it as if it did not weigh on me. Jacques's family values and my family values were not in sync or compatible, which would make raising our children in the future difficult. This was the first red flag that I decided to ignore.

Jacques-Laurent came to New York for a few days to date me. I picked him up from the airport, and my first reaction was that he had not changed a bit since I was seven years old. Only his hair was much shorter and a little thinner. He was dressed really well and used a lot of aftershave or perfume or something. We instantly clicked. We had the exact same sense of dry Dutch humor, and Jacques was just super kind. I am also a spontaneous woman with a lot of energy who likes to keep the house clean and organized. Jacques was the complete opposite and was constantly being thrown off by the hustle and bustle of New York City. Everything moved too fast for him, and there was too much going on around him for him to focus properly. I found this kind of weird but considering where we are from, I figured it makes sense. Only later did I find out that he was diagnosed as a small child with being on the spectrum. He was more of a calm type, very submissive, and a homebody who preferred comfort, peace, and quiet. I liked how he always gave in to my way, but this was because he believed more in me than in himself.

One bigger issue between us was Judaism. I was living a pretty religious life already at that point, and Jacques-Laurent never did anything with Judaism. During World War II, Jacques's grandparents were able to avoid deportation at the last minute by bribing a German guard with cigarettes. They survived the war working in factories with fake ID cards, hiding their Jewish identity. This secret that they had during the war carried on after the war.

They never spoke about their Jewish heritage, and Jacques was not raised with the idea of acknowledging it, let alone being proud of it. The neighborhood we grew up in encouraged this even more, as most of our neighbors still had that old-fashioned mindset. Despite this, Jacques was very much open to the idea of living a Jewish lifestyle, and we started by using his Hebrew name, Aharon. However, he wanted to do it for me, not because he necessarily wanted to himself. He really could not care less. It was painful to me how little he knew about Judaism and how rusty the basic Hebrew blessings were when presided by him. I was holding my heart, just hoping he would learn at least the basic prayers properly. He was willing to do and learn anything I wanted him to learn as long as I would not be disappointed in him. There was a lot of pressure in many areas, and I was scared that my mother would not approve. Adding to the already tremendous pressure, I decided not to tell my mother that we were engaged in the beginning.

I started to attend *kallah* classes, which are classes that a Jewish bride takes before she gets married. These classes prepare a Jewish bride for married life and teach them about themselves as women, their husbands as men, the intricacies of Jewish law governing marital relations, how to be a Jewish wife, relationship building, and how to run a Jewish household. Some *kallah* teachers teach more or go more in-depth on certain topics than others.

My *kallah* teacher was Mrs. Markovitz. An absolutely sweet, very short lady with a petite build, a high-pitched, melodious voice, almost like a cartoon character, and a little brown bob-lined wig with bangs. She was referred to me by the sister-in-law of the *Rebbetzin* from Upstate New York.

I don't remember why, but I visited the *Rebbetzin's* sister-in-law a few times in Brooklyn. Coming from such a big dynasty, she too was married to another big Rebbe, and they lived in Brooklyn like myself. This *Rebbetzin* was also a warm and sweet lady who supported me however she could. She sent me to Mrs. Markovitz, the *kallah* teacher.

Mrs. Markovitz and her family are Hasidic, but I would describe them as a little more liberal than most Hasidic families. All of their children married men and women who practice Judaism on different orthodox levels, based on the preferences and needs of their children rather than on their own personal preferences for what type of Jew they want their children to marry. Some of their children also have Hasidic partners, while others are married to a very orthodox person but not necessarily Hasidic.

I loved this. I loved how they respected their children for who they are and what they want and need for themselves as individuals, rather than what they want as their parents to keep up a certain image within the community, regardless of whether that's what their children want. I wish it were like this in every family.

Mrs. Markovitz lived in a typical, modest attached house in the middle of the neighborhood. The first time I met her, I couldn't help but notice how tiny she was. She greeted me warmly as if she knew me from before. Before we started the class, she told me about herself and her family, showed me pictures, and introduced me to her family this way, as no one else was home at that moment. Eventually, we went into one of her daughter's bedrooms to start the first class. I was directed to sit at a small desk across from Mrs. Markovitz. Thoughts ran through my mind: "What is she going to tell me that I don't already know?"

I'm from Holland, a super liberal and open-minded country, including in sex. I actually learned about sex and the whole reproductive system in school for a whole month. "I know what sex is. Is that what she is going to teach me about?" Yes, that was indeed what she was teaching me about, but there was so much more. Besides that, she was also teaching me how to properly take care of myself, my husband, and my household. Being a Jewish wife and running a Jewish household is not just a physical thing; it is very much a spiritual thing as well. The *kallah* class prepared me spiritually and mentally for becoming a wife.

As the information poured in, I realized more and more that my life was really about to change drastically. I had to give up many aspects of myself, and I would no longer be able to be this free child who did whatever she wanted, whenever she wanted and however she wanted. Laughing out loud in public the way Dvoire and I always did, rollerblading and ice-skating in public - many things were suddenly "not proper." I felt like I was losing myself, that I was getting conditioned, and I got overwhelmed. I started to cry. Mrs. Markovitz stopped immediately and felt so bad for me, even though she did not understand why exactly I was crying. She just kept on saying that marriage is a beautiful and holy thing, and once I am married, I will find that it is not so scary but rather joyous.

After a few classes, I started to ask some slightly rebellious questions: "Why can't I hold my husband's hand in public?" "Why must I be intimate with my husband whenever he wants to? What about what I want? And what if I just won't?" "Why this? Why that?" I kept on asking, but Mrs. Markovitz had the patience for everything and just the perfect answer for everything, sugar-coating it all, carefully making it look like my silly questions really were not so much of a concern at all. "I would want to be a good wife, so I would want to abide by all she is teaching me." I was carefully taught and eventually told myself.

After many classes and living in our culture on such a concentrated level day in and day out, I got used to the idea of being the perfect *heimisha* Jewish wife and everything that came with it. I convinced myself that everything she was teaching me was how it should be and how I wanted it to be.

I prepared my apartment for my soon-to-be husband's arrival. I purchased the perfect dishes for Shabbat with little pink flowers on them, two beds with typical pink bed linen, and two sets of white bed linen. I purchased the perfect long black fur-lined Shabbat coat with a mink scarf. Everything was "perfect." My neighbor's oldest daughter randomly started to want to help aggressively with everything. From the beginning, it just felt like she had nothing else to do, was just nosy, and loved to also be in the middle of all the attention this wedding between this dark Jewish girl and a random Jewish boy from Europe was getting. She wanted to know every detail of everything and would fiercely oppose if something was not according to how she felt it should be. She was also in contact with my *kallah* teacher, Mrs. Markovitz.

A few weeks leading up to my wedding, the big question of "are you really Jewish?" suddenly arose. This came up once Aharon and I tried to arrange a *mesader kedushin*, which is a Jewish marriage officiant. "Are you kidding me?" I asked. I have been discriminated against for being Jewish all my life, even by my own European Jewish great-grandmother, who is the reason why I was born Jewish.

Understand that as a child and in my teen years, I was pretty much alienated from Judaism and disgusted by the racism that my grandmother, mother, and I endured from my great-grandmother. Now I actually acknowledge my Jewish heritage to a very high level, and it is questioned if I am even Jewish? Aharon was in the same boat; he, too, had to prove that he was Jewish weeks before our wedding. It was the most stressful period of my life.

I did not even know where to start with proving that I was Jewish. How does one prove this? I had to be able to show that my mother-line is Jewish, that I am the daughter of a

Jewish mother, that my mother is the daughter of a Jewish mother, and so on. "What about my father? He is not Jewish," I asked sarcastically, knowing the answer already. It does not matter what your father is; as long as your mother is Jewish, then you are Jewish. Of course, I discussed this with my mother, and I was trying to conjecture why it is the rule that it does not matter if my father was not Jewish, only the mother. How unfair and insulting to fathers. My mother figured that this could be the rule because back in the day, during slavery in South America, Jewish men used to rape and sleep around and had so many children with slaves besides their own wives. All those "bastards" should be considered Jewish and treated as such?

Besides that, how would you know that the slave's child was conceived from Jewish sperm or that of the Christian English plantation owner next door anyway? With a Jewish mother, it is pretty obvious that the child is hers because the child comes out of the mother, therefore, unmistakably Jewish. Imagine what a "mess" it would be if every child that a Jewish slave master conceived by his female slaves would have to be considered Jewish? And how would it be proven which of the slave masters, their sons, brothers, fathers, male guests, and who else would be the biological father of a child between a female slave and a Jewish male in the first place? It was next to impossible in those days, not very honorable, and "not worth" the hassle, especially not for the child of a slave. Perhaps my mother was correct, maybe not.

I needed something - documentation, a Jewish marriage contract from my great-grandmother - something that proves that I am Jewish. My neighbor's daughter was driving me insane with this to the point that I started becoming rude to her, which did make her back off a little. Every day, she would ask me, "Did you find anything? Did you find anything? Not even a Shabbat candlestick? You must figure this out now!"

The Chief Rabbi of Holland got involved as well since I am from Holland. We had to follow my mother's bloodline and trace it back all the way to the mother of my great-grandmother by retrieving their birth certificates. This usually is a long and slow process, but for the right price and with the right connections, the people who work for the offices of vital records will speed up the process for you. I paid a huge amount of money to them so they would look into this matter immediately.

I received the birth certificates of the three female generations above me; the fourth one was born in Europe. The further up you go, the more Jewish it gets. It was super fascinating. On top of this proof, I contacted the German Synagogue in South America for records of membership of my great-grandmother and her family, but they were not able to confirm anything, explaining that most families that attended their synagogues were not necessarily members but of course, they have records of the family name. Custody records were found as well. When my grandmother passed, and my great-grandmother got custody over her granddaughters - who are my mother and my aunt - my great-grandmother's Jewish religion was mentioned in these records also, as she would further raise the children in the Jewish faith. With all this, I was able to establish my Jewish identity and "approved" to get properly married within the Orthodox Jewish faith.

My mother did not agree with this *shidduch* from the beginning.

"He is not for you; he does not have enough backbone, I am telling you."

She would tell me, knowing him for fifteen years herself. She did respect my decision to marry him and supported me throughout the process.

I made all the wedding preparations myself. Aharon was still in the Netherlands and would fly to New York about a week before the wedding. I chose a smaller, very nice, and fancy wedding venue that could hold 250 people, located in the middle of my neighborhood. The main ballroom had yellowish-golden colors with dark wooden accents. It was stunning. I decided on yellow flowers to match the colors of the hall. I would never choose yellow flowers for my wedding today.

I had the exact same wedding gown made for the ceremony as the queen of the Netherlands was wearing at her wedding. This dress was simple, white satin with long sleeves and a high bateau-shaped neckline. The train of my dress was 16 feet long, and my laced veil was 22 feet long and attached to my silver tiara, completely adorned with hundreds of crystals. It was magnificent. I wore my hair half up and half down. Extensions were added to make it appear fuller.

I did everything myself, and it was taking a toll on me. I was stressed, I did not eat, and I lost a lot of weight. I was seriously on the verge of collapsing from malnutrition and exhaustion. There were literally moments when my wedding guests from Europe forced sandwiches and yogurts down my throat. I was not only taking care of all the wedding details, including arranging all the flowers, but I also arranged apartments for everybody and was handling the food for the *aufruf* of my soon-to-be-husband. This is a ceremony in the synagogue held on the Shabbat before the wedding, where the groom is called to the Torah for a blessing called an *aliyah*. After, he is congratulated by the congregants, and the women will throw candy at him. After the prayer services, there will be a nice festive, fully catered *kiddush* luncheon.

A few days before the wedding, my two cousins arrived in New York to help me with whatever was needed. They are not Jewish at all and are as liberal and left-winged as a person can be. I had to drop off the packets with candy at the synagogue for my husbands-to-be's *aufruf*. My cousin Fiene was helping me schlep bundles of bags with candies and food to the synagogue, wearing nothing more than a tank top, jeans, and some simple slippers. I instructed her to put the bundles down on the ground outside the synagogue and wait outside while I brought it all in. She did not realize that I needed her to stay outside because of how she was dressed. She looked at me with frowned eyebrows and said, "Are you kidding me? Stop trying to do everything yourself, I am helping you." And she just waltzed right into the men's section of the synagogue while telling me this.

I tried to stop her, but she thought I wanted to stop her because I did not want to accept her help. But I really tried to stop her from going in because of how she was dressed, and besides that, we had to take the women's entrance, which was on the side. I ran to the women's entrance at the side and met her at the men's side again, where I found the very uncomfortable Hasidic Rabbi Klein. He did not know where to look and instructed us to just leave the boxes of candy on one of the long tables. I never explained to Fiene what the issue really was. Perhaps I should have, but I did not want to insult her either. Fiene was a tall and strong Dutch girl who just could tackle anything in no time with no problem. She was very strong.

My brother, mother, uncle, aunt, and nephew arrived as well. Fiene and her older sister Jette did not have dresses for my wedding yet. This, too, was something I wanted to control, as there were strict modesty rules for what they were allowed to wear at my wedding. Jette and I have been very close ever since we were kids. We used to do everything together; we shared the same principles and the exact same silly sense of humor. If there is something she would usually never do, she would make that exception for me, and vice versa.

We went to Manhattan to the garment district for dresses and shoes for my cousins and my mother. It was hard finding nice affordable modest gowns in gold-champagne colors, and I was just so exhausted that day - incredibly exhausted. At some point, we gave up trying to find modest gowns and purchased lighter gold-colored sleeveless gowns. The idea was to just wear long-sleeve shirts under them called "shells" in our community. These shells are specially designed to wear under garments to make them modest. For shoes, we just walked into some inexpensive shoe store and purchased somewhat comfortable matching shoes to go with the gowns.

Jette and Fiene would wear whatever I asked them to, as they really did not care what they would wear as long as I was happy. My mother, however, refused to choose some random cheap shoes from this store and demanded that we all go to Fifth Avenue to look for "proper" shoes for her to wear at the wedding. I refused and explained that I was tired and wanted to go home.

"Oh, now you found shoes for Jette and Fiene; you are all of a sudden tired? You had time to look for shoes for them, did you not? Now you are tired?" She asked.

"If you want to go to Fifth Avenue, you could go yourself. I am really tired and I have to go home." I responded while walking down the subway steps of 34th street in Manhattan.

Jette and Fiene stayed out of this argument; they didn't say a word and avoided eye contact with my mother. My brother, who came along looking for a suit, did tell my mother to leave me alone. She kept taunting me, and while we waited for the train at the platform, I just lost it and started screaming at her that I was tired and she had to leave me alone. After that, I burst out crying aloud, completely uncontrollable and unashamed of who was watching or what bystanders were thinking. I just had it with everything, and my mother's behavior was the absolute last straw.

My brother felt so bad for me and consoled me while scolding my mother for upsetting me like this. My mother was surprised by my breakdown and immediately felt bad as well. I don't think she realized how stressed out I actually was.

Before the wedding, I had to go to the *mikvah*. The *mikvah* is a Jewish ritual bath we immerse in to achieve ritual purity. I had hair extensions in my hair which all had to come out. Nail polish had to come off, and I was not allowed to wear any jewelry either. You have to be completely clean, natural, and rid of anything that does not naturally belong to your body, like jewelry, dirt under your nails, nail polish, food particles between your teeth, and anything that your body is about to shed, like loose hanging nails, loose strands of hair, dirt in your eyes, etcetera.

When I arrived at the *mikvah*, you would never guess from the outside of the building that you were about to enter such a spa-like serene place. I was the only woman there at that moment and was welcomed warmly by the lady who worked there. She explained the process. I was about to go into a bathroom to take a thorough bath, scrubbing every part of my body, washing my hair thoroughly, brushing my teeth, cutting my nails, and cleaning meticulously underneath my nails. After that, I had to brush my hair to make sure that I got rid of any loose hair strands. Once I was finished, I should put on the white bathrobe that was hanging there and then ring the bell. The *mikvah* lady would then come to me to check and make sure that I was completely clean.

Even though it was my first time in the *mikvah*, I was surprisingly comfortable with the whole process, maybe because my *kallah* teacher prepared me for this. Before I went to the *mikvah,* I was worried about it. "How clean will it be?" I was wondering the whole time. I have serious issues with dirty old bathrooms - they make me extremely uncomfortable and just cringe. When I book a hotel room, the first thing I always look at is pictures of the bathroom and the public's rating for cleanliness. When I look for a new apartment, it's the same thing. If the bathroom and kitchen are old and/or dirty, especially if the grout is dirty and moldy, then that is an instant deal-breaker. I won't take the apartment.

I don't know what I would have done if the bathroom at the *mikvah* was not up to par with my standards for cleanliness, but to my surprise, the bathroom at the *mikvah* was spacious and absolutely spotless, as if they had just renovated it. I actually enjoyed using this bathroom and took my sweet time preparing myself.

Once I was done, I put on the fluffy white robe, which was whiter than white, and then I rang the bell. The *mikvah* lady came to me and opened my robe to inspect my body carefully. She even checked for lint or dust particles on my body. After this inspection, I was led to the *mikvah*. Standing in that room gave me a feeling of ancient times as if it was not 2009. I don't really know why I felt that way. There were no windows, but the light that was shining there was that of the sky. The *mikvah* lady stood behind me and took off my bathrobe. I slowly walked down the steps into the pure *mikvah* water, expecting it to be cold, but it was warm and comfortable. I was standing across from her with the water up to my chest, looking up at her and waiting for her to instruct me further. She looked down at me and instructed me to immerse myself completely for a few seconds. When I rose back to the surface, I said a special prayer that was written on the wall and immersed myself again. The *mikvah* lady said out loud, "kosher!" when I rose back to the surface once more. She held the bathrobe open and up high for me to put it back on. I left the *mikvah* feeling super clean, both physically and spiritually. I truly felt like I had done what I had to do to have a pure, kosher, and holy wedding.

My wedding day was extremely stressful. I had no professional help and did everything myself with the help of my family. It was the dumbest decision I had ever made. I was the first one to go to the wedding hall because I had to get dressed in time to have pictures taken in advance before Aharon's arrival. My mother and cousins had to take care of some last-minute items for the wedding. I arrived around the same time as Aharon's stepmother, Ida, and father, Johan. His biological mother would arrive shortly after. I did my own hair and makeup, which was ridiculous. Ida helped me get dressed and keep my sanity. She was calm and treated me like a princess, constantly holding my train wherever I went without me even having to ask. She was catering to my every whim as much as possible, trying to keep me calm and happy. I was just tired and could not wait to get this all over with. I could not even fully enjoy this joyous occasion, which should have been one of the most beautiful days of my life. The photographer arrived beautifully on time and was organized and ready to go. I grabbed my bouquet, consisting of a mixture of cream-white Dutch and French tulips, which I had arranged myself. It was beautiful and exactly how I wanted it to be.

Me on my wedding day.

While the photographer was taking pictures of me on the elaborate stairs by the main entrance, my cousins arrived and were blown away by my transformation. Jette immediately ran up to me to hug me. Moments later, my mother walked in and got emotional.

Once I was done, I had to return to the dressing room immediately as Aharon was on his way. I had not seen or spoken to Aharon for a week, as it is our custom for a bride and groom not to see or speak to each other a week before the wedding.

My mother and cousins were in the middle of getting dressed. Jette and Fiene had not tried on the shell together with the dress before, nor had they thought about what they wanted to do with their hair and makeup. We just had some makeup for their skin color, which we had purchased at a local pharmacy and used that. I decided to do my mother and cousin's hair and makeup while dressed already in my crisp white satin wedding dress, not even nervous about getting it stained. They looked beautiful and appropriate for the wedding.

Aharon's biological mother was uptight and, unfortunately, not in the right and positive spirit at all. She is not used to openly being Jewish and doesn't say or do much. She was just there, moving along like a zombie, and that was it. I think that it was also hard for her to be around the current wife of her ex-husband, whom she still loved.

Aharon's step-mother Ida z"l and me.

Jette and I greeted each other upon her arrival at the wedding hall.

Me applying make-up onto Jette's face while Fiene is watching.

We could hear the guests arriving while we were in our suite. The one-man band arrived, and soft, casual music started to play while guests were talking with each other and laughing while enjoying the smorgasbord.

My cousins left the bridal suite to greet the guests, to make sure Aharon was on the men's side of the wedding hall, and to see if it was time for me to come out already. They pretty much came right back, letting my mother and me know that the hall was full and everybody was asking for me. They notified my brother, who then notified the Hasidic one-man band that the *kallah* was about to come out. This way, he could prepare himself to start playing a typical song played at Jewish weddings when the bride comes out.

We opened the suite door and made our way to the women's side of the ballroom. On our way, we ran into children playing on the stairs. They were gasping and looking at me in admiration while screaming my name. Even the responses of young children made me very shy.

As soon as we entered the ballroom, the music started playing with a much louder volume than before. My mother was holding my right arm, and my mother-in-law was holding my left. The women were all smiling and clapping to the beat of the music. Some couldn't wait until I was seated in my special chair and came right up to me to wish me and my mother *mazel tov*. I was overwhelmed with gratitude and joy at that moment. I could genuinely feel the love and positive energy coming from the guests. Everyone was just so happy.

My mother, Aharon's mother and me arriving and greeting the guests

My unmarried friends asked me to give them a *bracha*, which means a blessing. It is customary for a *kallah* to give blessings to those who are not married yet. My mother was sitting right next to me the entire time, observing it all, and was very proud. My mother-in-law was sitting next to me on my other side while my cousins were standing behind me.

A short while later, the volume of the music was increased again, and the next familiar melody started to play, a song called "Od Yishama". It was the melody you hear when the groom is on his way to veil the bride. I could hear the men singing the song to the melody, with trumpets following the groom. It was very intense, and all of a sudden, the energy around me turned much more spirited and emotional. I also started to cry immediately. "It is happening now," I was thinking.

Here came Aharon, led to me by his father and my uncle and surrounded by musicians and a large crowd of singing and dancing men. Aharon seemed rather abstemious but very happy to see me after a week of not seeing or speaking to me. His mother showed no emotion at all and looked rather frozen. She would smile at me quickly and politely every time our eyes met, but that was about it.

When he was ready to cover my face with the veil, he looked at me, smiling, and said, "Hi Sara," and started giggling a bit. He covered my face, and after that, there were a few recognizable male voices talking to me and blessing me before they left again toward the men's side, singing and dancing with the trumpeters following them. I couldn't see a thing, but I could hear the volume of the trumpets and singing descending as they left.

At this point, I was in my own world and taken away immediately toward the bridal suite with my mother, mother-in-law, and my two cousins. We stayed there until it was time to walk down the aisle to the *chuppah* I pulled up my face covering and sat down, staring at nothing. My mother asked me if I was ready to get married to Aharon. I looked at her, puzzled.

"And if I was not? Then what?" I asked my mother.

"Then you won't get married" she responded.

We were alerted to start getting ready by the entrance of the hall; it was almost time for me to walk down the aisle. My mother and Aharon's mother led me down the aisle with a burning candle in their hands. My cousins and the wife of Aharon's father were following us from a distance. My legs started to shake on my way to the *chuppah*, and I lost control of them for one second. My mother literally pulled me up firmly as if to tell me to "stop it."

When we arrived at the *chuppah*, the Rebbetzin from the synagogue I usually attended rolled up my train and pushed it into my mother-in-law's hands to hold on to while I walked seven circles around Aharon, with my mother holding onto my arm. I saw this later on my wedding video. My face was completely covered with a satin face veil, so I couldn't see anything and needed my mother's guidance in making the seven circles. Only later, when I watched our wedding video, did I see what exactly happened around me during the *chuppah* ceremony—who was standing under the *chuppah* with us, who was sitting on the first row, who in the second, who was standing on the side, who was schmoozing during the ceremony not paying attention, who was crying, and so on. I even learned weeks after the wedding that all the lights in the hall were left on during the *chuppah* ceremony while they were supposed to be turned off, except for the lights directly by the *chuppah*. I learned a lot from my wedding video.

Aharon walked down the aisle before me with his father and my uncle. He just walked as if he was walking to the bus station, then he stood under the *chuppah* waiting for me to come out, and also as if he was waiting for the bus. "He is so Dutch," I thought when I watched our wedding video—just so phlegmatic while I was the complete opposite, emotional, and in a very spiritual mood, talking to God the whole time. I did not feel like I was on earth at that moment. As soon as

Aharon broke the glass by stomping on it with the heel of his shoe, I woke up and was back on earth again. "*Mazel Tov! Mazel Tov!*" everybody around us screamed, and the festive music started to play again. My satin face veil was pulled up, and as dark, still, and quiet as it was before as if no one else besides the people under the *chuppah* were there, it was now loud, crowded, bright, and lively. "*Mazel Tov!*" with hugs and kisses from all sides.

The men started dancing in front of us again while Aharon and I slowly made our way to a separate room set up, especially for us to spend our first time together as husband and wife. The door was closed behind us, and we could still hear the singing and excitement outside of the room we were in. So, here I was with my new husband, though it was as if nothing had changed. It did not feel different, and we started to converse as we usually do—now about the wedding and the guests that were there and how it went on the men's side before the *chuppah*.

At some point, there was a knock on the door. I opened it, and there stood my mother. "There is a very special guest waiting for you by the stairs." "Special guest?" I thought. "Who in the world could that be? Probably somebody from Europe who came here to my wedding to surprise me!" I walked towards the stairs, and there was the *Rebbetzin* from upstate in a neat suit and silk headscarf, together with Mrs. Goldstein.

"*Mazel tov*, Sara, *mazel tov*," they said to me in a firm but very calm and formal tone while shaking my hand. I was very surprised to see them.

"Wow, you traveled at least two hours during rush hour to come to my wedding?" I asked. They softly laughed and responded, "You are worth it, Sara. How are you? You look so beautiful—wow, beautiful dress."

I apologized for not having my hair completely covered with a wig or tulle turban. In the Hasidic communities, it is customary to start covering your hair with a wig or a special white *kallah* turban right before you walk down the aisle to the *chuppah*. I had to go back to the room where Aharon was still waiting for me. They served us dinner, but I was not hungry at all. I took a bite here and there while chatting with my new husband, who was very hungry. After dinner, we were taken away to another separate space to take pictures together and with the family. Before we knew it, we had to go back to our guests to dance.

There were already kids by the door calling us to come out. All the hard work and emotions from the day drained a lot of energy out of me. I was exhausted and asked myself how I was going to dance all evening long. It seemed impossible. The music started to play louder and in a rousing tone, indicating that Aharon and I were about to come out. I ran out into the ballroom on the women's side, and my mother met me immediately to dance with me first. I was excited and found new energy to dance. The women started to dance in circles around us. After my mother, I danced with my mother-in-law, who all of a sudden seemed to be much happier and more comfortable than before. My cousins came next, and after them, the *Rebbetzin* followed by Mrs. Goldstein.

I just always love to dance. If someone were to put a hidden camera in my house, they would find me laughing, singing, and dancing most of the time whenever I am on my feet, and some sort of music is playing. I literally twirl like a ballerina from the dining room to the kitchen most of the time, and I don't know why. I just love dancing, and I am always happy to dance, especially at my own wedding. I was so tired, that there were moments when I had to sit down for a few minutes. The women would dance in front of me to entertain me whenever that happened.

Sometimes I was brought over to the men's side too. It is not suitable for a Hasidic woman to dance in the presence of men, but I just could not completely hold still on the men's side while the music was playing, and all these men were dancing with such passion in front of us to the music that reached my soul to its core. My head and my fist swayed to the beat of the music.

I had been to many weddings but never witnessed the "acrobatic tricks" that the men did at my own wedding. Some were flat-out dangerous, and sometimes I was about to jump up to put a halt to what they were doing. One guest put his hat on fire, and another guest put someone else's son on a chair and then balanced the chair on top of his head! This child, whom I had known since he was a baby, made me so scared, but he loved it and gladly participated in this "trick." He was sitting in this chair with a fearless and smirked look on his face while his side curls dangled all around his head as the man below him tried to keep the boy balanced on top of his head. There were other men standing close by in case the chair with the boy in it fell.

After all the dancing, most guests left, and only my closest friends and family stayed for the *mitzvah tantz*. Since my family is not as large as most ultra-orthodox families, and no one in my family is religious in the first place, our *mitzvah tantz* was small and short but meaningful.

Me, walking down the isle with my mother and mother-in-law

Me getting entertained on my wedding on the men's side.

Jette, Fiene and I dancing

The wedding was over, and I couldn't wait to sleep. Aharon and I stayed at a luxurious hotel on Fifth Avenue and 59th Street in Manhattan. Our suite had a black, white, and golden interior and a separate sitting area. The bathroom was spacious, a rarity in Manhattan, and had beautiful, high, crown-molded ceilings. We were welcomed with a personal, handwritten congratulatory note on the table, along with some non-kosher chocolates and champagne. I was so tired that I couldn't even enjoy the fancy amenities of the hotel. We could have stayed in a one-star hostel with bunk beds, and I wouldn't have cared as long as I could sleep. I took a shower and crashed instantly. I felt terrible for Aharon the following day. He wasn't involved in any of the wedding preparations and had all the energy in the world. All he had to do was buy his own Shabbat and wedding garb and a new suit. He didn't even make sleeping arrangements for his side of the family.

I went around viewing and renting sublets for his family and stocked them with fresh, crisp white towels, linens, food, and drinks. I wanted to make sure that these apartments were spotless and that their stay was perfect and comfortable. While I was sure that my linen and towels were fresh and clean, I wasn't sure if and how the linen and towels left in these sublets were washed or what else they were used for previously. The linen and towels that came with the sublets had random colors like navy blue, brown, or maroon. I wanted them to be stark white, crispy, and clean, just like in a hotel.

Married life

It was now time for *Sheva Bruches*, or as most people pronounce it, "*Sheva Brachot*," which means "the seven blessings." During the seven days following our wedding, Aharon and I were treated like a king and queen. Elaborate dinner parties were arranged as part of our tradition. Each night, we went to a different location - some nights at the house of a close friend and other nights at a restaurant or the small "party hall" of a *shul* (a synagogue). It was important that each time, there were at least ten men present to form a *minyan*. A *minyan* is a quorum of ten Jewish men required to perform Jewish communal worship. I was incredibly tired, and all I wanted to do was stay home and rest on the sofa in a comfy robe with my new husband, but that was not an option at this time.

Every evening, we showed up dressed to perfection in the stiffest silk outfits, the most uncomfortable patent-leather heels, and the itchiest stockings. I wasn't used to wearing a wig. The bangs that fell on my face annoyed me, and the wig sat heavily on my head at first. I did feel gorgeous but very uncomfortable. It was unbelievable how our friends went all out to make every evening so special for Aharon and me. This was the first time that I didn't have to be on top of anything related to my wedding. I just had to show up, and I was tremendously grateful for the efforts my friends and family made for us.

After the *sheva bruches*, Aharon stayed in New York one more week before he had to go back to the Netherlands to wrap up some personal business. He still had an apartment there which he also needed to rent out. I stayed behind, feeling weird. I really had to get used to all the drastic and definite changes in my life, and interestingly, how these changes got once again disturbed abruptly with Aharon going back to the Netherlands.

I looked at myself, "I am married now, but I live alone," I was thinking. It got all of a sudden very quiet around me. As lively as it was before and as much attention I had received only up to a few days ago, right then, it felt like all that had never happened. As if it was a dream.

My entire family went back to Europe, Aharon left as if it is normal to do that right after your wedding, and I also felt very much alone all of a sudden. There were two beds in my bedroom, men's clothing hanging in my closet, and silver kiddush cups in my little breakfront, but there was no husband. So, what am I now, then? There is stuff belonging to a man all over my apartment, yet, I don't live, and I have never lived with a man before, so I did not have the feeling that I was living with a husband, especially since I have never experienced this. It felt weird.

This wig also; I had a hard time getting used to it and wore a *tichel* most of the time instead, which is a head scarf.

I started to lash out at Aharon over the phone.

"Why did you not take care of all this before?! How come you are only taking care of this now? What do you mean you have to work more in the Netherlands? Why did you not save any money before? Which man with a job that only had to take care of himself doesn't have any savings? Why did you marry me if you did not have your business

216

together? Why this? Why that? This is really not normal! You are not normal, Aharon!"

He felt my stress and started to travel back and forwards a lot to be with me. When he was home, all was well. We went out most of the time on Shabbat and holidays, and we were just the perfect little *heimishe* couple dressed, behaved, and lived accordingly.

At some point, we decided to eat at home on the evenings of Shabbat, which is Friday evenings, unless we had a special invitation for a celebration or something. I loved our Friday nights. It was just relaxed and intimate.

The house would be extra clean. I loved that the world didn't expect anything from me the following day, and I could sleep in a little bit as well. I always set our table for two and would make fish, soup, and potato kugel. I usually bought chicken, different kinds of salads, dips, and whatever else caught my eye in the store and looked interesting and yummy. Aharon loved to drink beer on Friday evenings after our meal, so that would always be on my grocery list as well.

The *challah*, which is traditional Jewish braided bread, is often homemade by Hasidic women, but I would buy it every week from a specific bakery in Borough Park that sold a lot of other goodies as well. The bakery owner was very friendly and always happy. His whole face would smile when he smiled, and I got to know him pretty well, I guess. He reminded me of Ari a lot - very Hasidic, overweight, big-mouthed, and loud. You could hear his laughter throughout the bakery. He would always have a few of his younger children hanging out in the bakery, and would always chat with every male customer, and end the chat with something funny, followed by loud laughter and "Gut Shabbos!"

When he spotted me in his bakery, he would nearly scream, "*Suri imeini*!" which means "Sara, our mother," or he would say, "*Rebbetzin*!" I would just smile and nod at him, quickly acknowledging him while feeling a bit shy.

"Vus darfst die Rebbetzin vus darfst die hant? Wie viel challahs? Drei? Drei medium sesame? Vus nuch?" He would say. Which means "What do you need, Rebbetzin, what do you need today? How many challahs? Three? Three medium sesame? What else?"

When I was finished with my order, he would often come up with some new specialty.

"Rebbetzin, I am going to put this in your bag also. You have to try it. The dough we use now is so much flakier, you know? Try it, and tell me what you think. If you don't like it, I am not selling it anymore."

I am sure he was joking. He would talk so loudly and with arm gestures that I often felt embarrassed not knowing how to respond.

"Okay Mr. Oberlander, but I am paying for it, yes? I am not just taking it." I responded.

He would tut his tongue in disagreement, open and extend his hand my way while telling me nonsense really as to why I was taking it now and why I am not going to pay for it.

"How much do you charge for this?" I would ask.

"I don't know. Gut Shabbos Suri imeini!" He would scream happily and move on to the next customer.

Sometimes I would estimate the price myself and give it for *tzedakah*, which is charity. One time, I took it out of the bag, put it on the counter, and left the bakery. Mr. Oberlander noticed it, and while I was walking away, he called me back, but I kept walking. The week after, he would say that I really insulted him and stuff. Sometimes I would have him deliver my order. I would text him what I needed, and he would have it delivered. Sometimes he had questions about my order when something was not in stock that week or something. His question would always start with "*Suri imeini?*" followed by the question.

I told my husband at the time about Mr. Oberlander and the way he talked. He did not say much in response, but when he saw the text message with me being referred to as "*Suri imeini*" by another man, he got very upset, accusing Mr. Oberlander of liking me too much, which might have been true, but I really don't think so. He was not secretive about calling me "*Suri imeini*," and he himself had an interesting and rather flamboyant personality in the first place. He called me "*Suri imeini*" in front of his own children. Aharon messaged Mr. Oberlander behind my back, threatening him that if he contacted me one more time, he would let everybody know that he liked me and was behaving inappropriately toward me. Mr. Oberlander responded simply with, "I am sorry; I don't want any problems."

Aharon told me this after Mr. Oberlander texted him back, and Aharon was very proud of himself for being able to "get another man to back off" so easily. I was not happy with this.

I felt like Aharon was too quick and aggressive with his message, and he should have discussed this with me first instead of secretly threatening Mr. Oberlander. He is a good man. He might say some things that he should not say, but I really don't think that there were any ill, destructive intentions there. Aharon could have told me to ask Mr. Oberlander not to call me "*Suri imeini*" anymore, and that would probably have been the end of it in a much more peaceful way with no hard feelings.

Every Friday evening, I would wear my comfortable black velvet, lace-adorned Shabbos robe with my white turban and my *sheertzel*, which is a delicate white lace apron. We had a small, simple table that could seat no more than four people comfortably, six people at the very max, with barely any room left to move your arms comfortably. While Aharon was in *shul*, (the synagogue) I would light the Shabbat candles, start to set the table, and read the weekly Jewish magazines and newspapers I had picked up earlier that day. Besides some greatly entertaining stories and recipes, I always learned something new and wise every week from the writings of different *Rebbetzins* in these magazines and papers. Sometimes I would fall asleep while waiting for Aharon to come home from *shul*. The evenings of Shabbat were and still are always the best moments of my week. Sometimes it happened that Aharon unexpectedly would bring home a guest or two to join us for the meal. I always had plenty of potato kugel, challah, and salads, but I had to halve the fish but I did not ever mind.

I just loved this spontaneous side of Aharon and really appreciated it when guests gave me compliments on my cooking. I really never learned how to cook from my mother.

My father used to cook most of the time when I was a child, and in my head, I didn't really know how to cook interesting and varied dishes. I also almost never follow a recipe precisely and add ingredients to a dish by feeling, just hoping it will turn out to be something more interesting and better than if I had measured out all the ingredients exactly as described in the recipe.

I was also slowly getting used to wearing a wig, but only in combination with a scarf or headband to keep the hair out of my face. Sometimes I would only leave out the hairline of the wig and cover the rest with a silken head scarf. This is a common way for ultra-Hasidic women to cover their heads as well. Some people found it funny that I would leave the hair of my wig out sometimes and almost completely cover it with a head scarf other times. It is very uncommon for a Hasidic lady to cover her head in different ways in public. You usually cover your head one certain way and that way only, usually the same way your mother covers her head or an extra step further to appear even more pious than your own mother. I always covered my head based on how I wanted to cover it that day. The more layers I would use, though, the "older" I would feel and look. I felt mostly like a young, refreshing bride with just a wig.

Me, during the first year of being married.

Bubbe Glick

Soon after I got married, I got very bored at home and decided to look for a part-time job. I had this idea in my head that I could not work full-time, being a devoted *heimishe* wife now, even though my husband was in the Netherlands most of the time. I started to read the classified sections of the newspapers on Saturday evenings after Shabbat. I did not even know what kind of job I was looking for. What I did know was that I did not want to work in an office again at that moment, and the job location had to be close to home, preferably within walking distance. I was surprised by how much there was a demand for caregivers for children with special needs. There was one advertisement that stood out to me: a family is looking for a young Jewish female to make meals for their elderly mother and to keep her company. "I can do that," I was thinking. Their mother lived in the middle of the biggest Hasidic neighborhood in Brooklyn, only a 20-minute walk from my house. This is perfect!

When I called the phone number, I spoke with the oldest daughter for a while and was invited to meet her and some of her siblings in person. I remember wearing a black dress with a white blouse under it with its collar sticking out. My wig was perfectly styled, and eventually, during the first few months of my marriage, I managed to find comfortable heels, which I wore to this meeting. I felt confident as if I owed the world, and it rubbed off because I was hired within ten minutes. We did have a little disagreement about the salary.

"Will the 400 dollars less really make or break it?" The oldest daughter Clara asked me about my salary.

"You really don't have to do much. We have a housekeeper who cleans my mother's house every week. She has a caretaker who comes every morning to wash my mother, and she does all the heavy work. You only have to keep her company and cook for her; that's it!" Clara finally said.

Of course, this sounds very light, but I know that it would not be as "light" as it sounds. She was asking me to be responsible for an elderly woman who has a hard time moving around.

"Okay, I understand what you are saying, but imagine, what if one of your grandchildren goes to visit their *alte-bubbe*, (great-grandmother), they use the restroom and make a mess. Do you then expect that I wait for the housekeeper to come and clean it up and to let your mother sit on this dirty toilet? Or would you expect me to be mindful enough and clean it up first? It sounds very simple, but the job goes beyond just keeping your mother company. I have to be responsible for her and her well-being. I am sure that this is what you would expect from me, no?" I explained.

Clara sat at the table and rested her head in her hands while looking at me in despair as if what I was asking for was tremendous and nearly beyond her. I looked back at her, smiling but did not budge.

"You are right, Sara. Fine, we will pay you what you want. When can you meet me again at my mother's house?" She finally responded.

Bubbe Glick - just saying her name and thinking about her now moves me to tears. Bubbe Glick was an old, rather tall Hungarian lady in her mid-eighties with strawberry blonde hair, and hazel-green eyes. She really was an absolutely stunning woman with elegance, morals, and self-respect. We shared the same birthday, she was my height, and even though she never wanted to leave the house, my goodness, that woman always dressed up as if she was going somewhere major. Gorgeous silk blouses with perfectly tailored designer skirts and matching jackets. Her wigs were styled like Queen Wilhelmina of the Netherlands herself.

Bubbe Glick was a Holocaust survivor who went through a lot, and the Holocaust made her a tough woman. Behind all the wealth, perfection, beauty, and smiles was, unfortunately, a deep-seated sadness and pain completely unprecedented to me. Bubbe Glick lost many family members to the Holocaust, and it was as if she could and would not permit herself to be completely happy. As if she "did not have the right" to be happy because many of her family members had not been lucky like her and perished during the war. When there were moments of laughter, she would laugh for a slight moment and then would quickly remind herself to mourn instead or something.

There were random moments when she would tell me snippets of stories of her childhood in Hungary and what she went through during the war. I later understood from her own children that she never told them anything about what she went through, which is something I hear a lot from other families as well. There was this one older sister Bubbe Glick had whom she just adored so much and was very proud of and felt she owed her life to.

"My sister saved my life... she saved my life... Sara? Did you hear me? My sister Miriam, she saved my life in Auschwitz," she would repeatedly tell me in Yiddish with a thick Hungarian accent.

"During selection, I was selected to go to the gas, but my sister quickly pulled me out of the line when the Nazi was not looking."

Bubbe Glick would tell me this every so often as if she had forgotten that she had already told me that quite a few times before. She would make heavy gestures with her arms and hands while trembling. I respected her a lot and would listen every time as if it was the first time she told me this story. I just never knew how to quite respond to this tragedy that happened to her, and I would just listen, slightly shaking my head in recognition.

Sometimes I would carefully ask questions to try to understand better what her experiences in the camps were. She would pour out information like a waterfall and then all of a sudden stop as it all of a sudden became too overwhelming for her. "I don't want to talk about it," she would say while her eyes would fill up with tears, and making a dismissive motion with her hands. Days later, she would tell a story again; most of the time, it was a story she had already told me. I don't think that Bubbe Glick ever received professional help or guidance to aid to process what she went through. It seemed like she just had to deal with this trauma by herself, and sometimes it was just spilling out.

Bubbe Glick had six children, all living in different communities in New York. They were all married and had larger numbers of children themselves and even grandchildren. They would visit their grandmother often, but Bubbe Glick did not seem to ever truly enjoy this. She would tolerate it but nothing more than that. I probably enjoyed having her grandchildren and great-grandchildren around more than she did. She would often not know who is who of her younger grandchildren either. Her great-grandchildren were even a bigger "mystery" to her.

She had different bonds with each of her children. I could tell that the relationship between her and her oldest daughter, Clara, seemed a little strained. There was barely any love between them, and Clara explained at some point how her mother would never express any emotions towards her. She never expressed how proud she was of Clara or how happy she was for Clara, not for anything, not even at Clara's wedding.

Bubbe Glick's youngest son, Shulem, was her baby and her world. He had the most children out of all his siblings and happened to be the smallest also. Bubbe Glick just adored him. He probably got spoiled much more than the rest of his older siblings. He acted spoiled, also.

All the siblings communicated on a regular basis, had agreements in place for their mother, and some sort of a system for money, how they would rotate visits, and taking her for *Shabbossim* (plural for Shabbat) and to appointments. Shulem did not pay any mind to any of these rules or systems, and did not necessarily agree with anything. Nobody had to tell him anything about how to handle "mamie" and everything involving her, especially not the wives of his brothers.

"If mamie wants to take a two-hour nap in the afternoon, then let her take a two-hour nap; please, don't listen to Gitty; she is not the boss," he would tell me.

"If mamie wants to eat the whole box of chocolates, I brought for her, then let her enjoy it; tell Malky that I said she can if she has anything to say about it."

He would literally tell his sisters-in-law to mind their own business sometimes. Despite all this, to me, he was the most pleasant and relaxed sibling to have around. He was very friendly and kept the vibe refreshing when visiting. He could chat about light and fun stuff, completely unrelated to the care of his mother, making her feel like an active part of society and making me feel more like a family-friend, whereas his siblings would be much more focused on the business aspect of my presence when they would come over. Talking about medications, "yes" to daily walks, "no" to long afternoon naps, next week's doctor appointment, "did the *goite* (housekeeper) come this morning?" And Shabbat plans for "mamie". And I only had to cook for her and keep her company? I felt like a personal assistant sometimes, on top of being a cook, but I cared for her deeply and did not mind it.

Bubbe Glick had one older brother and one younger sister herself. The rest of her siblings were no longer alive. Her brother's name was Karl; we would call him Uncle Karl. Uncle Karl lived in Canada and was in his nineties but had energy like a forty-year-old. He would visit his sister on a regular basis and drove all the way from Canada to New York to visit her. Sharp as a whistle, he was a very tall man with a loud and clear voice, no hair, and thick glasses. Uncle Karl was not as soft-spoken and emotional as Bubbe Glick. His character was much more outgoing and adventurous.

When Uncle Karl would tell me stories about the war, he would speak in a way that was like he was telling a big, exciting action story with good guys and bad guys. Uncle Karl is tall and used to be blonde with blue eyes, so he portrayed himself as an Aryan boy during the war and was part of the Hitlerjugend. He would tell me how his "Aryan peers" would stand and listen like brainwashed zombies while Hitler was speaking during the Nuremberg rally, which he attended as part of the Hitlerjugend. "As if they saw God himself!" he screamed in excitement. He would mimic their faces, opening his mouth halfway and his eyes wide open while staring into the distance in amazement. "It was unbelievable. I have never seen anyone respond to a person like that, ever!" he would tell me, still surprised himself. Sometimes Bubbe Glick had a hard time listening to her brother's stories. Bubbe had a completely different experience during the war than he did.

Half a year into my marriage, I got pregnant. Even though I wanted to have a baby, I cried as if the world was ending when I found out. "What am I going to do? I don't know what to do!" I was sobbing, even though I had taken full responsibility for Alisa like she had been my own daughter for years.

My mother was ecstatic and laughed instead, saying, "Well, *mazel tov*! Don't be so silly. You will be fine." Aharon was also happy and acted like we had already had ten babies before this one.

Bubbe Glick's daughter-in-law, who I had gotten pretty close to, responded with, "Don't worry *mamele*. Whatever you do, just don't drop the baby, that's all." I was thinking sarcastically, "Really (not) funny and great advice." Her point, of course, was that everything would happen naturally and would fall into place on its own. Your mother instinct will tell you what to do and when to do it, and as long as you don't drop your kid, you will be fine.

I arranged for an obstetrician right away to get all the testing done and instructions to follow with regard to vitamins, do's and don'ts while pregnant, and such. After the initial shock, everything seemed rosy to me until I was given a Pap smear. This experience was so painful and unpleasant that, to this day, I have never taken a Pap smear again. During the rest of my pregnancy, I was very careful about any other procedures my obstetrician wanted to do and wanted to know every detail of what my obstetrician wanted to do to me before she did it. I would not let her stick anything inside of me anymore. I could not trust her anymore.

My belly grew fast, and I became proud of my pregnancy. As scared as I was before, I was excited now. I was pregnant like billions of other women but acted as if I was the first pregnant woman ever. Around seven months into my pregnancy, I vigorously organized and cleaned my house in preparation for the baby's birth. I had three strollers, and I knew everything about every stroller. I could tell you from a mile away which stroller was approaching, from which brand, which version, and what the pros and cons of that stroller were. The same went for baby bottles and pacifiers. I lived my life for my husband and baby, and took family life very seriously.

During the summer, while in my third trimester, I had a hard time getting around because of the heat and humidity. The sun just sucked the little bits of leftover energy right out of me, and I was prone to fainting when walking outdoors in the heat for an extended amount of time without liquids. Coca-Cola and iced tea were my best friends! A month before my due date, I was on my way to Bubbe Glick's house. Usually, I would walk to her house, but with this hot, humid weather and being so pregnant, I had to take the city bus. While waiting for the bus, I started to feel weaker and weaker and had to go back home before I fainted again. I called Bubbe's daughter-in-law, Gitty, and explained that I was not able to go to Bubbe's house today. Gitty responded,

"I just think that this is it. You are almost having the baby, and you need to take it easy and rest for the remainder of your pregnancy." She responded. She was totally right.

The birth of my first child

My mother came to New York to support me during the last few weeks of my pregnancy and the first two weeks after my baby was born. She was very excited and so happy and grateful that she was able to be with us during the birth of the baby and help us. "I did not have that when I was pregnant with Miriam," she reminded me. Miriam is my older sister, and my mother did not have her mother to be there with her during labor, and support her during the first few weeks of having her first child. In my little one-bedroom apartment, she slept in the living/dining room, and I slept in my bedroom with my husband. I knew what I was having and shared this information with my mother. My mother brought a lot of expensive clothing for the baby from Holland. It is our custom not to buy any clothing for a baby before it is born, but this is not something my mother will listen to.

One night, around 2 am, I heard something in my kitchen. I jumped out of bed to investigate, and as I jumped, water started gushing down my legs. My water had broken, and I was in labor. To my surprise, I did not panic. Instead, I grabbed a towel and tried to clean up the water while holding another towel between my legs to prevent any further mess. Aharon, had slept through all of this.

As the pains of labor started to intensify, I decided to wake up my mother. I opened the living room door, and she woke up instantly.

"I think I'm in labor," I told her in Dutch.

"You're lying," she replied in disbelief while getting up.

She rushed towards me and saw a trail of water on the floor. "Your water broke? When did your water break? Why didn't you wake me up right away!"

Aharon woke up also, and I went to lie on the couch with a waterproof pad underneath me. Every so often, I felt an intense contraction, but my instinct told me that it wasn't yet time to go to the hospital.

My mother wanted to help so bad, but there was nothing she could do at this point, of course.

Around 5 am in the morning, the contractions were coming every ten minutes or so, and I decided that it was time to go to the hospital. Aharon called a regular cab, and we were brought to the hospital.

At the hospital, they installed me in a very nice suite, spacious and with two comfortable couches that turned into beds if needed. It seemed like I was in labor forever, I was dilating, but the baby just would not go down the birth canal. It turned out that my pelvic bones were too narrow, the baby could not fit through, and therefore, they needed to do a cesarean section to get the baby out.

I was lying there in a bright room with about eight nurses surrounding me. They all minded my body and each other, but none of them really minded me as a person, as a mother in labor. I felt like a piece of meat.

My mother had to wait outside, but Aharon was sitting right by my head, trying to encourage me, I recalled. However, I could not stand the smell of his breath. My sense of smell was very sensitive during my pregnancy.

After a short while, I could hear a little baby crying. "It's a boy!" the nurses were happily screaming. "A big boy you got, mama!" This was the first time during the procedure that they spoke to me. My son weighed nine pounds and six ounces. They showed him to me, and he was indeed this big, fat baby boy with a round body and a round face. He looked at me as if he knew exactly who I was and what I was all about. His face felt very warm, much warmer than my own, and so soft and delicate. I was absolutely over the moon.

Naturally, I had to stay in the hospital for a few days after having a C-section. The room they transferred me to after the baby was born was not as nice as the first one, and I didn't like my nurse. She was cold, impatient, and not gentle enough. At some point, I had had enough and pulled out all the cords that were attached to my body. "I am going home," I said to myself. I could barely move but managed to get myself, and the baby dressed carefully. The nurse caught me and started screaming at me with a thick Russian accent.

"You cannot do this, madame! You cannot pull out the IV! What if we have an emergency and have to give you medicine now?!"

"I don't care!" I screamed at her.

"Do not dare to touch my baby, you!" I said angrily with my eyes wide open while pointing my finger at her.

She looked at me for two seconds and then quickly ran out of the room as if she was scared for her life, only to return with, I believe, a head nurse.

Upon arrival with the head nurse, the Russian nurse started to raise her voice, complaining about me. The head nurse sent her away, realizing that her presence would only escalate the matter. The head nurse started to talk to me in a very calm, sweet, and understanding tone, explaining that it was in my and my child's best interest to stay one more day. I would get another nurse and another room with a bed next to a window so I could actually get some daylight. I agreed to stay for one more day in a new room with a bed next to a window. The rest of my stay was pleasant, and I was treated like an actual human being who just gave birth to a baby, instead of like a piece of unimportant meat that needed to be processed quickly.

The following day, my son and I were discharged from the hospital. Aharon came to pick us up and brought a car seat for the baby. His little shoulders were so broad, they filled the entire width of the seat. "Oh! He is going to be a football player!" some nurses said.

When I arrived home with the baby, I was desperate for a good shower and my own bed. My mother had cleaned the house thoroughly, put fresh flowers, little "welcome home!" balloons, and "It's a boy!" tchotchkes everywhere. She meant well, but all those different colors and extra stuff lying around made me feel like my house was disorganized, and it made my head spin. Everything was washed, sterilized, set up, and ready to be used for the baby. The baby was happy, comfortable and slept all day.

My mother took care of him more than I did the first few days. I could tell that she had raised quite a few kids and knew exactly what to do, when to do it, and how. Aharon helped as much as he could, but he was a little overwhelmed by everything and cracked easily under pressure. The lightbulb in the hallway ceiling lamp had burned out quite some time ago but was never changed. I asked him sarcastically if he had not noticed that the light was not working because the lightbulb needed to be changed.

"Yes," he answered, agitated, knowing very well where I was going with this.

"Well, then, why haven't you changed it? I was in the hospital for three days; why haven't you changed it?"

Then he asked me, "Well, you also noticed that it was not working, right? So why have you not changed it if it bothers you so much!"

I just stared at him in disbelief for a few seconds and then responded, "Well, uhm, let me think about this, oh! Maybe because I was nine months pregnant, you moron! Do you really expect me to climb on a ladder to change the lightbulb in my condition?"

Aharon walked away to take a walk outside to cool off. He was stressed out, and this disappointed me. If he was stressed for the well-being of the baby and me, it would be one thing and more acceptable for me. But he was stressed because of how everything had changed, and he did not know how to adapt to this new life change very well.

"Why is he stressed? For what?" I was thinking. I was the one whose body was taken over for nine months. I was the one who was in labor for a day and a half, stressed out because my pelvis bones were too narrow for the baby to pass through the birth canal. I was the one who lay down on a table while they cut me open to take the baby out, and now I was in pain, could barely get up by myself, and could barely walk. I was the one who gave birth to a baby. I was fine, the baby was fine, and my mother helped us with everything. Why in the world was this man stressed? For what?"

"Maybe he just needs some time to adjust to this whole new situation, and this is his way of adjusting." My mother said.

"And try to be a little gentler. This might help." She concluded.

When Aharon came back, I was sitting on the sofa in the living room with the baby sleeping in my lap. The kitchen is right at the entrance of the house. My mother was cooking, so she was able to take him aside before he would come to the living room and see me. I don't know what she said to him, but even before he came to the living room, he changed the lightbulb in the hallway and then proceeded to the living room. He took the baby, sat in front of me, and apologized. I was so disappointed and did not respond.

The baby was almost a week old, and I had to go to the doctor for my postpartum appointment. I was doing and feeling much better and walked around as if I had never given birth, doing my usual things. My mother insisted that I leave the baby home with her while Aharon and I went to the doctor.

"He is too young and should not go out right now if it is not necessary." She said.

I left the baby with my mother, and Aharon and I went to the doctor's office.

When I came back home, I expected the baby to be missing and needing me desperately or something. We walked into the house, and I asked my mother right away where the baby was. "He is sleeping," she answered super calmly in a slightly whispering voice. I went over to his little crib, and there he was. My mother had given him a bath and put him in a cute heather-gray one-piece outfit that she had brought from the Netherlands. She brushed his hair to one side like a little nerd, and he was sleeping so peacefully, not missing me at all.

It was a busy time as we prepared for the traditional circumcision ceremony for our son, called a *bris milah*. Close friends of ours, Mr. and Mrs. Jacobovitch, generously offered to host the whole ceremony at their home, and also provided all the food and drinks for our guests. All we had to do was arrange a *Mohel*, the person who performed the circumcision, and we had to arrange the flowers. They even arranged a photographer, a mutual friend of ours. I searched long and hard for the perfect traditional white silk outfit for my baby to wear with a matching pillow for him to lay on during the ceremony. The idea was to keep this outfit and pillow in our family for the rest of our future sons, grandsons, and great-grandsons to wear during their *brisses*. I found the perfect little set in a simple store where you would not expect to find such an outfit. It was a beautiful white silk-satin pillow with silver engraving, a matching silk-satin one-piece outfit with short sleeves, a matching cook-like hat, and a long white "overcoat" that went over the one-piece, looking like a regal mini *beketcha*.

But I was stressed out because it became real to me that someone was about to cut into the foreskin of my son's penis. I started to think about it a lot, and asked myself many questions. All these questions ran through my head throughout the night and the day of the bris. I invited many friends, and Mamie Farber also came. Aharon and I were running late and headed to Mr. and Mrs. Jacobovitch's house in a rush. As I got out of the car with the baby and started walking towards their house, I could already hear the men from a small distance, and I became more nervous. All of a sudden, I saw someone's side curls dangling over the balustrade of the front porch of the house, followed by a head that looked straight at us. He pulled back quickly, only to return with a few more men looking over the balustrade, motioning towards us to hurry up. One of the men was Mr. and Mrs. Jacobovitch's oldest son. I wanted to turn around just to breathe for a minute, but my mother did not let me, of course. Aharon was intimidated by those men rushing us and just passed me by and rushed towards the house as the men instructed, not noticing my stress. The *kvaterin*, which is like a Jewish grandmother, took the baby from me as soon as we entered and she passed the baby on to her husband, the *kvater*. While he walked away with the baby, he was praying and made gestures to reassure me that everything would be fine without breaking his prayer.

The *Mohel* wanted to speak to me briefly to make sure I followed his instructions beforehand and to make sure everything was all right for the rest. I was already crying from being nervous and afraid. The female guests all greeted me with big smiles, happily and warmly, but I was so nervous and just wanted to be where the men were with my baby.

Mrs. Jacobovitch asked me why I was crying and told me not to worry, as if I was being silly. "Why are you crying, *mamele*? Do you think that your *yingela* (little boy) is the first *yingela* that gets circumcised?" She laughed to lighten me up and embraced me to comfort me.

Everybody tried to calm me down and distract me, but I was extremely tense. Even my mother tried to make me feel better while she was clearly nervous herself. "This is exactly why mothers don't go to the *brisses* of their own babies; we just can't handle it!" Mrs. Jacobovitch said aloud to the female crowd.

At some point, the *Mohel* circumcised my baby, and the baby started to screech right away, of course. A real heart-wrenching cry. I cried immediately also and started heading towards the men's side while everyone was saying, "*Mazel tov! Mazel Tov*! Yehoshuah-Alexander! What a beautiful name!" Yehoshuah-Alexander "Shea'le" or "Yehoshealexander" when I pronounce his full name in Yiddish. The *Mohel* had put a piece of cloth, drenched in red wine, in Shea'le's mouth. He was sucking desperately on it, really trying to get the most out of it. Just the fact that Shea'le was quiet and seemed content, and I was holding him again, changed my mood instantly. I became approachable again and posed happily for pictures.

Shea'le and me on the day of his circumcision.

Shea'le five months old

Shea'le during his haircut ceremony

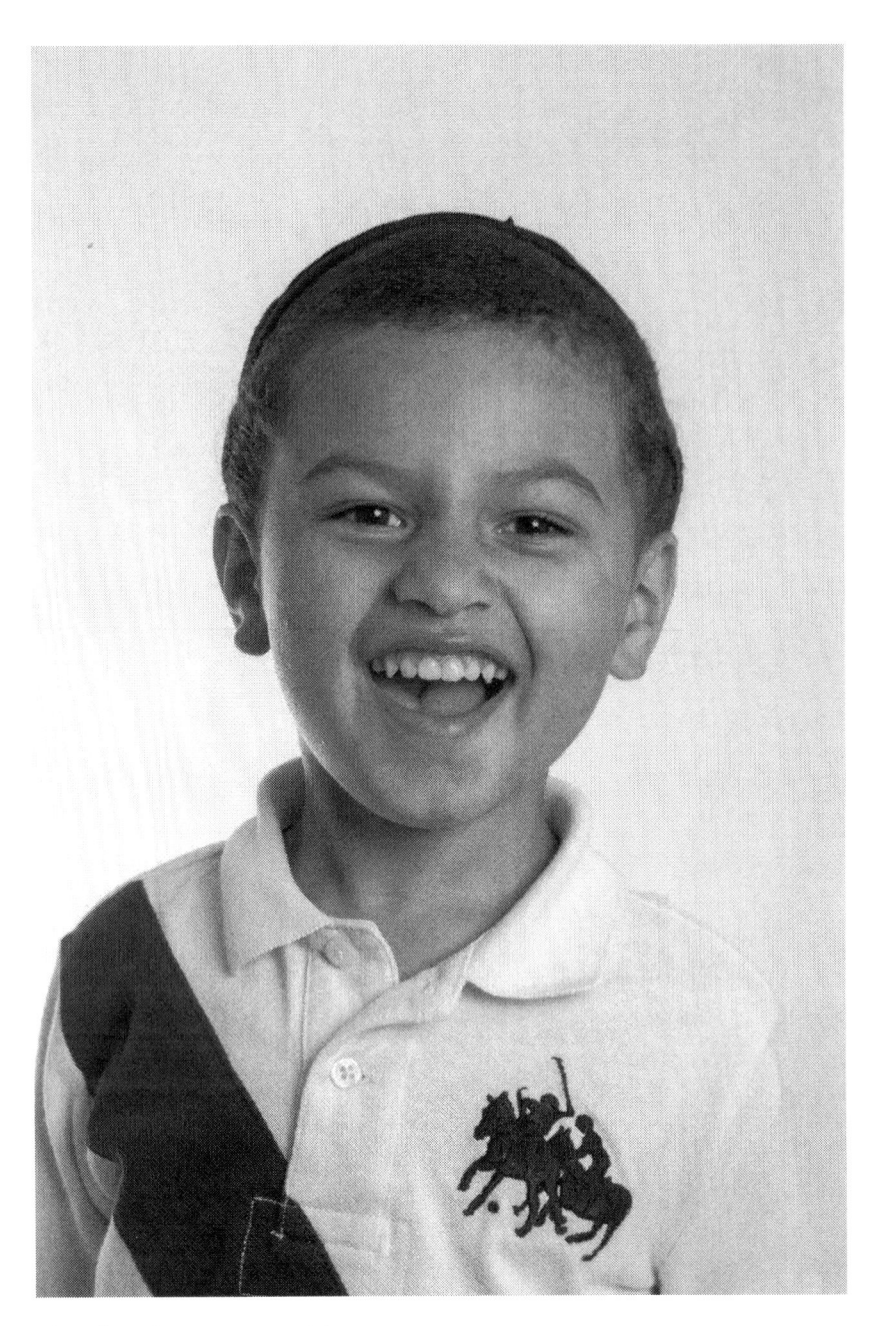

Shea'le, three years old

Shea today

It's amazing how a mother's instincts kick in once she has a child. My sleeping habits changed instantly as soon as I became a mother. As deep as I slept, I was always on high alert and could hear everything. If Shea cried, most of the time, I knew exactly why he was crying. I could even recognize the slightest adjustments that needed to be made for him to stop crying and be happy again. I must admit that often it was just a hug or the sight of his mother that would make him happy again. Shea was very attached to me, and I was very protective of him, perhaps too protective, as he was my first child. I was insane and overdid almost everything. I had four different strollers lined up in my kitchen for this one baby.

My first and main stroller was large and very comfortable, with a spacious, cushy seat, endless reclining options, an extra-large sun canopy, and a large basket underneath for groceries. It was very comfortable to push, and I used it almost every day to run errands in the neighborhood. Then we had an "umbrella stroller," which was much more compact, folded, and unfolded easily with one hand, and we sometimes used it when taking the bus or train with Shea, along with a baby carrier in case he did not want to sit in his stroller. We also had a "snap&go" stroller specially designed to carry car seats. It was a compact stroller frame that we could snap Shea's car seat onto. We used this stroller when we went somewhere by car, especially in taxis. Finally, we had a beautiful white leather stroller with a white furry seat that we used on Shabbat and holidays. This stroller cost us a fortune, and with a baby in it, it was an absolutely beautiful sight to see, especially when the baby was dressed in white also. However, it was not very comfortable to push.

Shea had more than he needed, along with a mother who would respond to his every whim. I loved parading around with him on Shabbat while he was dressed in his finest clothes and presented in his fancy stroller.

The birth of my second child

The following winter, when Shea was four and a half months old, we were in the midst of moving to California to try and see if we liked it there, despite everybody's recommendations. I found that my life was getting too dull and I was looking for a change with a little more diversity and excitement. There is a beautiful large Jewish community in Los Angeles, with plenty of Jewish schools, clean streets, sunshine, and beautiful exotic trees. "Sounds just perfect, and who does not want that?" I thought. Well, I was wrong and definitely did not think this plan through thoroughly enough before pushing my ex-husband to agree for us to move to California.

I underestimated the distances from one place to another in Los Angeles, the cost of living there, which was higher than what I am used to, the ways of life, and myself, living there. Our lives, especially mine, were so deeply seeped into the New York Hasidic lifestyle that I was not able to find myself devoting and living in an environment like California full-time and forever. I even missed the four seasons, and overall, I missed the Jewish spirit in the air that New York has so strongly.

On a Friday afternoon in Brooklyn, New York, you feel that it is the evening of Shabbat. Everything screams it and moves towards it. I would make my Friday morning walk to Thirteenth Avenue in Borough Park, Brooklyn. On my way to Thirteenth Avenue, I would smell a mixture of potato kugel, cholent, and laundry detergent the entire way coming from the houses I passed. This particular mixture of different scents is symbolic of "home" and "erev Shabbat" to me. It seemed like nobody cared for Shabbat or potato kugel in Los Angeles, just sushi and freaking kale salads. It seemed like nobody was busy with cleaning and preparing for Shabbat except for us, while most of my neighbors were Jewish. I would leave my doors and windows open and would cook and clean so vigorously that some of my female neighbors would sometimes watch and ask questions.

All of a sudden, I would see a skinny blonde lady sticking her torso through the door.

"You use a mop to clean your floor? Oh! Doesn't it damage your floor?" she would ask.

"No, of course not. Just make sure that you don't leave puddles of water lying around. How else am I supposed to wash the floor? How do you do it?" I would respond.

While distracted by all the silver, prayer books, and Shea, she would answer, "I use a Swiffer, much easier, leaves no stripes, and it cleans really well."

"How wonderful, well, that must do," I would think sarcastically. Without making eye contact, I would just nod my head, not wanting to explain how I don't believe that Swiffer is the solution for properly washing your floor. Maybe for a quick "in-between mopping" clean-up, but not to get your floors actually seriously clean.

She would continue to talk and make funny faces at Shea for a few minutes and then say, "Well, Shabbat Shalom!"

The following week, another blonde would stick her head through the window and say,

"That smells delicious! Is that uhm,... What is it called again with the shredded potatoes? Oh yes, potato Kugel! My bubbe used to make that when I was a kid; she would shred the potatoes by hand, too; it's delicious!"

"did your mother ever make it? What would you have for supper on Fridays?" I would ask.

She would look at me with a big grin while thinking about those "good old days."

"We did not have a big Shabbat meal every Friday night, you know? Sometimes my mother would light candles but sometimes not. Pretty much depended on my father's work schedule, but my mother would not make kugel; she would order food and make a salad to go with it or something."

Again, I would not make eye contact and just nodded my head, not wanting to give away how much I felt about how disconnected this woman was from Judaism and the value and importance of Shabbat.

Eventually, I would respond with, "Come back in two hours, and I will give you a potato kugel if you want." The following week, another neighbor would pop her head into an opening of my house and ask, "Aren't you hot in that long dress? It is so hot today!" and so on. Every week there were these questions and remarks. Most of my neighbors and I were living in two completely different worlds and had completely different priorities. "How am I ever going to make friends in this place?" I often wondered.

I was pregnant again and had a rental lease for a year. If it were not for those two things, we would have gone back to New York right away. Of course, there was a Chabad house where we often went, but the overall crowd that went there also, was not my type of crowd. 95% were at least 20 years older than me, and most of them had their own specific, interesting custom ways of observing Judaism. I was not willing to be open to their unusual ways and to stray in any way from our *heimishe* way of observing Judaism. Of course, today, I believe that everyone should just live and observe however suits them best, but back then, I would silently strongly disagree and would have nothing much to say to you.

My ex-husband, however, navigated comfortably through this interesting crowd and was able to make quite some friends. I felt alone and could not connect nor comfortably root into Los Angeles. I must say that I did enjoy the beaches, the shopping, the privacy, and the space I had. I am the type of person that likes to pull away from the world sometimes and be one with nature and my thoughts. I had a hard time doing this in New York but not in Los Angeles. The beaches stretch for miles and miles with no person in sight. The sunsets are breathtaking. I would just walk or lay in the sand with Shea while talking to the universe.

I was very pregnant and got bigger and bigger. The bigger I got, the less I could walk, of course. Aharon had to go almost everywhere with me at some point because I could not carry anything. One morning, I needed to go to the grocery store, but Aharon did not want to get up yet to go with me. I had no patience and decided to go by myself, using the stroller as a support to lean on.

On my way back home, I started to feel dizzy and unstable. I knew this was not good. My legs started to shake, and I had to sit down. I was in the middle of nowhere, and there was nothing to sit on, so I sat on the ground, leaning against a huge rock that was bigger than me, breathing heavily and getting in and out of consciousness while trying to hold onto the stroller so no one could move it. Shea was sleeping, but the fact that I would not be able to do anything for him at that moment, really scared me a lot.

I don't know how long I was lying there, but at some point, a fancy white sports car stopped right next to me. A middle-aged lady jumped out and frantically started to ask,

"Oh my God! Are you all right, my dear? What happened? Are you okay? Are you hurt? Were you hit by a car? What happened?"

"Just dehydrated," I responded weakly.

"Bruce! Bruce! Bring a bottle of water, please!" In no time, I had a bottle of ice-cold water in my hand.

"Take some! Drink!" The lady was ordering me.

Instead of gulping the much-needed water down, I decided to see if the bottle was sealed first. If it was not sealed, it could be that it is not kosher. The lady thought that I was looking because I had a hard time figuring out how to open the bottle.

"Oh, of course, I am sorry. I'll help you. Here, here, please drink." She said.

After I drank some, she quickly took a look at Shea but brought her attention right back to me when she realized that he was sleeping peacefully. Her husband was standing behind her, observing the situation, and ready to do whatever his wife asked of him.

"I live right down the street. Let me take you to our house. I will make a nutritious smoothie so you can get your strength back, okay?" She said.

Before I got a chance to answer, the lady screamed, "Bruce! Help me pick her up, please!" While they wanted to pick me up, I said, "I can go home. My husband is there. Thank you so much for the water."

"There is no way you can go home by yourself in your current condition." The lady responded.

In the background, her husband was shaking his head "no" in agreement with his wife. The lady putted her hands underneath my arms.

"We will bring you to your house. You cannot go by yourself. Bruce, help me, please, honey." She said.

I was very uncomfortable with Shea being outside of the car while I was already inside.

The lady picked up on this immediately and took Shea very carefully out of the stroller, and sat next to me with Shea in her lap, still sleeping. The car was nicely air-conditioned, and immediately I felt that I could breathe better.

Her husband tried to fold the stroller up to put it in the trunk, but he was not able to do this, and after a few minutes, he exclaimed, "Suzanne! Please help me here; I can't get this thing to fold down."

Suzanne looked at me and said, "Don't worry, I will be right back. Are you able to hold the baby, or should I lay him next to you?"

Of course, I told her that I could hold him, so she gave him to me, and she went to help her husband. The cold water and air-conditioned car made me feel much better in no time. I could feel my eyes opening up more and more, and I started to take a good look around me.

I could hear Suzanne struggling with the stroller.

"It has been ages since we used one of these; how do you fold this thing?

Oh no, now the seat has come off. Did we just break it?" Bruce said.

"No, I think it is supposed to come off first, actually." Suzanne responded.

Eventually, they figured it out and slammed the trunk shut in relief. Suzanne sat next to me in the back of the car, and without asking, she took Shea out of my lap and held him while we drove. They typed in my address on their "car computer screen" and drove up to the gate of my apartment complex.

Our apartment complex was gated, and I did not know the code by heart, because we did not have a car. I felt so much better and convinced Suzanne that I could walk to my building. Suzanne walked with me while her husband, Bruce, stayed in the car, waiting for her to come back.

I rang the bell, and Shea woke up in the meantime. Aharon, still in his pajamas, opened the door and was very surprised to see me standing there with a stranger next to me.

"Hi, I am Suzanne, my husband and I don't live too far from you guys. Your wife fainted in the street; we found her half-unconscious, so we brought her home." Suzanne said in a very friendly tone.

Now Aharon looked not just surprised but also frightened, and while we usually speak Dutch to each other, he asked me in English, "Oh no, are you alright?" I looked at him, probably with an annoyed expression on my face, and said in a dry tone, "Yes, I am fine now; please help me with putting these groceries away."

He was embarrassed and obviously could feel that I was not happy. He started to unload the stroller immediately, not saying or doing anything to possibly upset me any further. I turned to Suzanne and thanked her for her wonderful care and the lift back home.

There was silence between Aharon and myself. A few minutes later, Aharon asked me, now in Dutch, while slowly unpacking the groceries, "Why did you not wait for me to go with you?" This question made me boil, but I tried to stay polite and responded with, "Because it was already 10:30, Aharon. How much longer was I supposed to wait?" I asked, agitated.

He could not answer, and there was silence again. A few moments later, Aharon asked, "Why did you not wake me up then? You could have woken me up, you know? I really would not have minded."

Now it was harder for me to compose myself, and with a raised voice, I said, "I did, Aharon... if you would not be on your laptop all night long, maybe you would be able to get up at a normal time, or at least remember what you said to me when I tried to wake you up at 10:30!" Aharon said nothing more.

A few days before my due date, my mother came to California to help us with Shea'le and the household. She could sense immediately that things were not the way they were supposed to be. I felt unsupported by my own husband. I felt like we were living in two different worlds and had different priorities.

I experienced how my ex-husband was rarely able to properly evaluate a situation and respond accordingly. Like something was off with him, and I often had no patience for this. I felt like I did not have a man, and I just simply needed a man, more of a resilient and supportive man with some discipline. He was not that and would not even try. Just as my baby Shea'le needed guidance in everything, Aharon needed guidance in everything, and I often had no time for this. I often wondered if he was mentally okay.

Then during some random conversation about the schools we went to as children and teenagers, I came to find out that he went to a school for teenagers with slight disabilities. I was happy that I had an answer to all my concerns, but at the same time, I was disappointed that he had never told me this before and that I had never paid close attention to this before we had children. When it was just the two of us, everything was fine and normal, but as soon as there was more going on than usual and the pressure was on a little bit, it was as if Aharon got overstrung on an abnormal level that just would make my eyebrows raise.

My second child was born at UCLA in California. Another huge 10.6-pound boy! This one had exactly my facial features when I was a baby: a big forehead, chubby cheeks, and round pouting lips. His colors, however, were completely different from mine and also Shea's. This baby was a full-fledged blonde baby with blue eyes for the first few months. And everywhere we went, somebody had something to say about it. "Is this your baby? But he is blonde!" As if I did not know. His bris was held at the Chabad House of Malibu. It was a much more relaxed experience compared to Shea'le's bris. But even over there, we were confronted with remarks about the baby's coloring. One of the shul-goers even said, "His older brother is so much darker; I think this baby will have a much easier life." I was stunned by this remark, although later in their life, I did learn how my blonde child received so much more attention than my darker child.

Shea'le, one year old and my second son, a few months old.

, the *mohel* (the person who performs the circumcision) frustrated me a bit. We agreed on one price, but as soon as he saw my lavish mother entering the Synagogue with a classic jumbo Chanel bag on her shoulder, he tried to nearly double the price for his services for some bogus reason. "I would have gladly paid that price if we had agreed on this price from the beginning, but not like this; we agreed on a price already," I told him.

Then he tried to make me feel bad by saying, "Okay, if you think that it is the honest and right price to pay, then so be it." I stuck by our initial agreement and paid exactly what we agreed on.

I was not as much of an emotional mess as I was with Shea'le's bris, probably because I had been through it already and knew that my second baby would also be just fine. The atmosphere was also not as heavy, which helped a lot.

"Moshe Ziesman" is the new baby's name. We call him "MoisheZies" or just "Moishe." In Holland, everybody calls him "Moeshee," no matter how often you correct someone. Very interesting. Soon, we started to give him the nickname "Sushi" because that is what Shea'le called him, not being able to pronounce "Moishe."

Moishe as a baby with his older brother Shea'le

Moishe as a toddler

Moishe almost three years old

Moishe at Shea's haircut ceremony (upsherin)

Moishe during his haircut ceremony.

Moishe, 4 years old

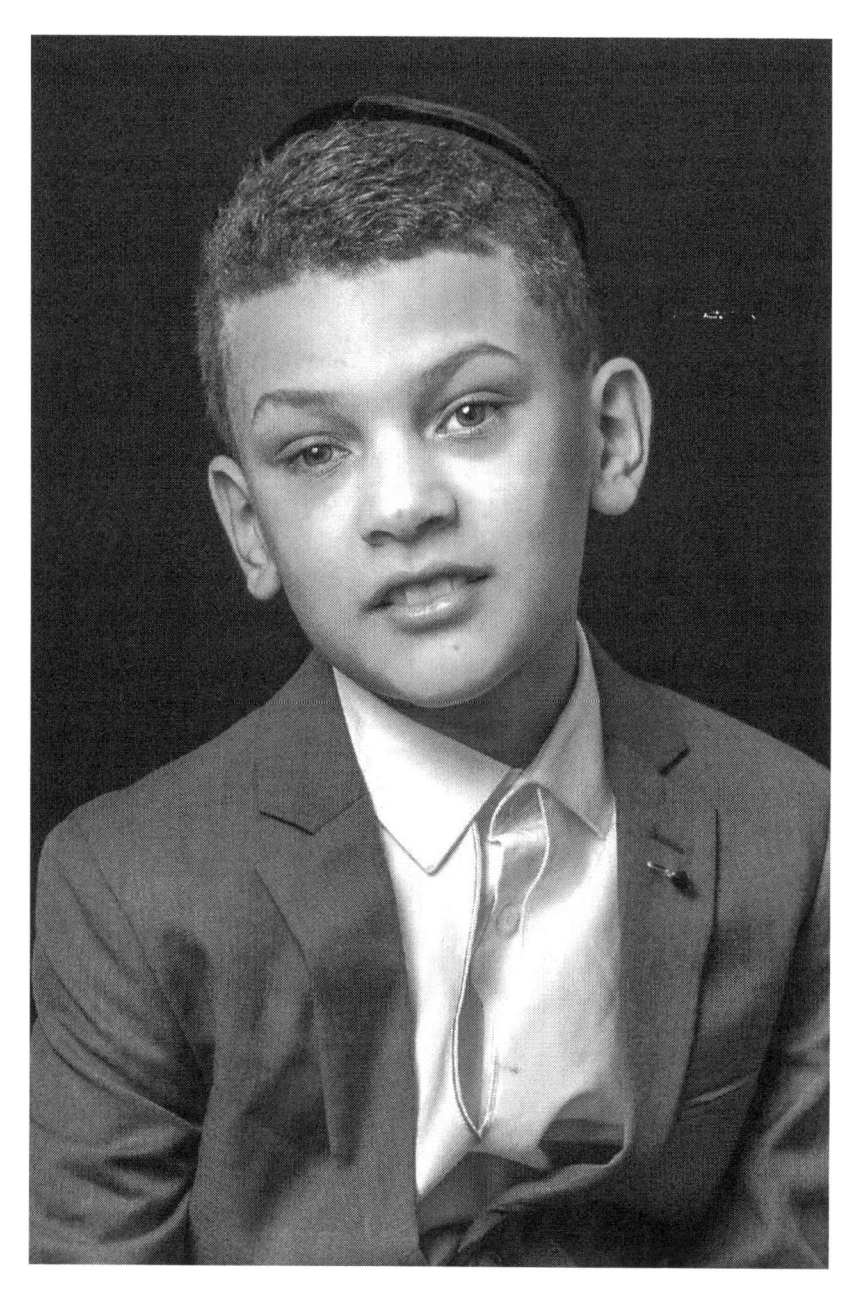

Moishe today.

In the beginning of 2014, I gave birth to my third son Meijer, pronounced as "Meir."

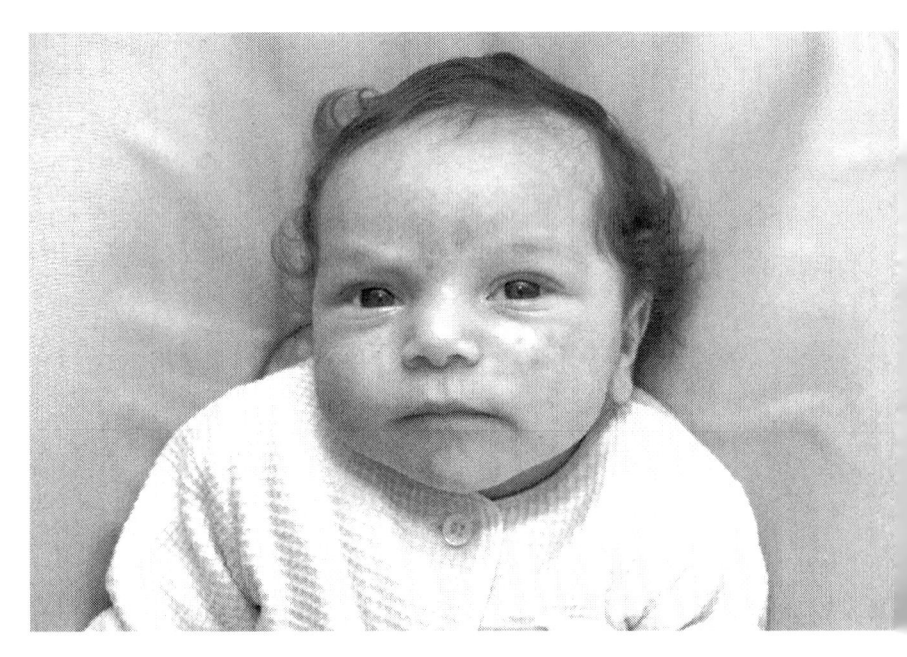

Meijer two weeks old.

Meijer on the day of his haircut ceremony

Meijer three years old

Meijer five years old.

Meijer today

Shea'le and I in Los Angeles.

Back to New York

I just couldn't take Los Angeles anymore. I missed my friends, I missed winter and autumn, and the overall heimishe atmosphere that hangs in the air in New York like nowhere else. While sitting in my Malibu condo surrounded by all these gorgeous blonde, skinny, youthful "babes," I was fantasizing about a nice, spacious, "shoe-box" shaped apartment on Ocean Parkway in Brooklyn, surrounded by other heimishe Jewish and probably Russian neighbors. Los Angeles was just not the place for me. We packed up everything and moved back to New York when Moishe was only one month old. Aharon went along with the idea, seemingly not feeling any certain type of way about it.

It was dark, cold, and rainy when we arrived back in New York, and I just loved it. It felt cozy to me. We rented a small sublet in Williamsburg, Brooklyn, for a month, which was exactly the time it took for our furniture and other belongings to arrive from California to New York. While we looked around for an apartment around Kensington and the east side of Borough Park, it seemed like we would never find anything we somewhat liked, and it was quite a trip to go from Williamsburg to Borough Park for every viewing with a baby and a very young toddler. But despite all this, I was just happy to be back in New York, to finally have a "real intense Shabbat" again.

Newspapers and magazines with new apartment rental listings would only come out once a week, so every time we viewed all the apartments, we had to wait a week again for a new batch of apartments to view. Towards the end of the second last week in our sublet, we went to see an apartment on Ocean Parkway. This apartment was exactly what I had in mind in Malibu. A large shoe-box-shaped apartment with a ton of daylight, two spacious bedrooms, and a clean and up-to-date bathroom and kitchen. We were led inside the apartment by one of the maintenance guys who instructed us to just close the door behind us when we were done looking around. As soon as he left, Aharon and I looked at each other, knowing from each other that this was it. This is the apartment we were looking for.

I let Shea'le walk around to see if he was comfortable in the space and see how he would move around, and I sat Moishe in the stroller in the middle of the dining room with some music playing. They also seemed very comfortable. I really tried to create the energy of that apartment being ours already. I started to wash Moishe's milk bottle and made a fresh bottle of milk in the kitchen as if it was my kitchen already.

After the application process and an interview with the building's board members, we were approved. We were so happy, and I felt like I could breathe again. The first thing I did before our belongings arrived was hiring a company to have the carpets professionally cleaned. There was a beautiful wooden floor underneath the cream-colored carpets, but we were not allowed to remove the carpet because, as per New York City law, 80 percent of apartment building floors must be carpeted or something.

We started to see our friends again while getting our apartment together.

I was in my element! Shea'le was about two and a half years old when I started to look for a *cheider* (a school for Jewish children) for him. Of course, this *cheider* had to be something like "modern Hasidic" or something - a *cheider* where Hasidic children from different Hasidic backgrounds go, perhaps sprinkled with a few *Yeshivishe* children (non-Hasidic orthodox children from families with strong connections to the orthodox Yeshiva world), and where the mothers and fathers tend to be more open-minded in overall.

Of course, I did my research way in advance and knew exactly which schools I would apply to and then be done with that. This was so much harder than I expected. These Jewish schools tend to be very much into keeping a certain image and reputation and will only accept certain types of children from certain types of families. They even asked for information about the grandparents on the applications which at first made me wonder why, "what do they have to do with this?"

Aharon and I are *Ba'al Teshuva* (Jews who used to live a secular life and now live a more orthodox life). My wig was often considered too long, my sweaters too fitted, I wore make-up, both Aharon and I come from this "random place in Europe, right next to Germany," we have no family in the US they could connect us to, and I had an iPhone which was a huge "no-no". On those applications, you specifically have to sign off on not having a television and a computer in the house where the child you are applying for lives. Some schools will be okay with it if you have a computer for work purposes only and also in a separate room in the house that is to be locked at all times. The computer needed to have a filter on it also. Hasidic schools found us to be too modern, but *Yeshivishe* schools found us to be too Hasidic. It seemed like a school that was suited for our children did not exist. You could not necessarily label us as other frum families, and every Hasidic school catered to certain Hasidic labels. We were and still are pretty random observing Judaism how it works for us.

Back in the day, almost every European Jew could speak Yiddish, but today, in general, only Hasidim speak Yiddish. We speak Yiddish at home, we are *heimish*, but I allow my children to watch certain videos. I wear fitted tops sometimes and would not mind looking a Hasidic man in the eyes when I speak to him, or he speaks to me. Certain things that we do are considered "uncomfortable, unusual, sometimes even inappropriate" or "don't match with mainstream Hasidim." "Why don't you apply at Chabad?" (a certain Hasidic community that tends to be more modern and open-minded), many would ask us. "Because we are not Chabad," I would answer. We are not from a specific Hasidic branch, we are just us.

I started looking into smaller schools as the bigger, well-known schools with excellent reputations just seemed too rigid and impossible. Aharon could not care less where Shea'le would go to school. He was not interested in learning anything and strayed more and more from *Yiddishkeit* himself, which bothered me tremendously.

I found a small, simple advertisement for a small Hasidic school in one of those weekly Jewish magazines I would always pick up. I did not know exactly what to expect and was worried about it being a stiff, sterile "makeshift basement school" that was academically probably far from up to par with the city's mainstream elementary schools, but I went to take a look anyway.

The school for children until the age of five was located on the edge of Borough Park in an adorable townhouse. The classrooms all had a warm, sweet, and colorful atmosphere, and there was a diverse group of Hasidic female teachers with varying styles of head coverings, from longer wigs to short wigs to headscarves with black or nude ties. I loved the variety.

The head of the school was a Rabbi and his wife, and I mostly dealt with his wife, who was a knowledgeable Hasidic lady with excellent English-speaking skills. Rabbi and Mrs. Glauber welcomed Shea'le without any judgment or hesitation, accepting us as *heimishe* Jews without scrutinizing our background.

The school was small, and there was strong communication between the staff and parents. As Shea'le had always been home with me, this school was a perfect starting point for him. I was thanking God that the big prestigious Hasidic schools didn't work out, as this small school was ideal for the time being. I knew that when Shea'le turned five, I would start worrying about where he would attend next.

Shea'le making a painting in school with Moishe next to him

Shea and Moishe waiting for the school bus.

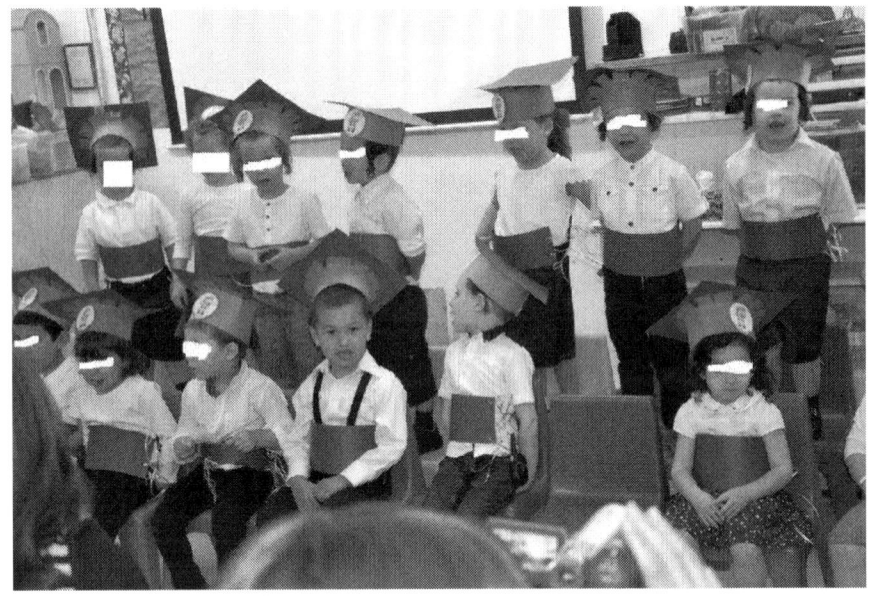

Shea'le during his class graduation ceremony.

Shea'le after his graduation ceremony at school.

Conclusion

Everything was perfect except for Aharon and me. We were more like good friends who got along well instead of husband and wife. Too often, I was secretly thinking about what the best option would be for me with regard to how to continue my life. I knew that this is not how a marriage was supposed to be. I wanted more than just a nice friend who often lacked basic common sense and who needed so much guidance constantly. I already have friends, very good friends; I wanted a husband. A husband that sometimes supports me, not even always, just sometimes.

It was very hard for me to feel for him like a wife should feel for her husband after everything he has shown me through our marriage and after everything I came to find out while we were married. Aharon had a very light form of autism which came to light during our marriage. I was secretly running scenarios through my head while also telling myself that marriages are just never perfect and they do always require work. I did not want to say anything out loud, scared that I would create something that I was not certain about and not ready to create. I told myself that Aharon was at least a good man with a good heart who never acted violently toward me or ever used profanity.

None of my friends had a better marriage than we did, some even worse with no affection whatsoever, but their marriages were rather "family trades," at least; that is how it seemed and felt to me sometimes. It barely matters if the boy likes the girl or vice-versa, as long as they can tolerate each other; what matters is which family he or she comes from, what their reputation is, and position within the community. When somebody gets engaged, the first question will always be, "to the son or daughter from which family?" "The family" is important. For me, however, this is much less important than the man I am actually marrying himself. Who is he? Who is he as an individual? Are we even compatible? What is he all about?

Currently, I am divorced, and not so long ago, a *shadchan* (Jewish matchmaker) suggested a particular young man from a perfect family. He was from a certain Hasidic community that I have very close ties to myself, and like myself, he was described as somewhat more open-minded. He had eight siblings, of which each and every one was already married, except for him. The reason why he was not married yet, being the middle child and the only child of his parents who is not yet married, was so vague that at that moment, I pretty much already knew that something must be going on. Especially because this family does not personally know me to just randomly agree to an interesting case like me.

"The family is wonderful; the family is so wonderful!" The *shadchan* was saying.

When I asked around, the family was indeed described as being wonderful. "Nice well-known people with 'good money.'" They say.

"Why is it that they are interested in me if they are so typical and perfect? I am very unusual, why was I suggested?" I asked the *shadchan*.

Without answering that question, the *shadchan* asked me to just give it a shot and speak to the young man in question.

The young man was a very lively person with an upbeat voice and a kind but audacious and supercilious character. Ten minutes later into the conversation, I understood very well why he was not married. He might have been of an adult age, but his way of thinking and talking was very immature, like that of a twelve-year-old. Something was seriously mentally wrong with him, and I knew right away that he was absolutely and definitely not going to be my husband, posing as a father-figure to my children. I do not care how wonderful his family is.

During this first conversation, he asked me when we would meet but, in my mind, this conversation was already over and done with, so without thinking, I asked; "Meet? For what?"

"We need to get engaged, no? Or do you want to get engaged over the phone? Hahaha!" He responded.

I told him that I would speak to the Shadchan about this. After this conversation, he kept calling. Sometimes he would fill up my voicemail box with him just singing the *Yiddishe* songs that he wanted to know if I liked. I told the *Shadchan* that he was not for me and explained why. The *Shadchan* "had no idea" that there was anything wrong with him and only heard good things about him and his family. She did pass my rejection on to his family, but he would not stop contacting me.

At some point, I figured that perhaps he needed to hear from me why I was not continuing with him, which was definitely not the smartest configuration. At first, he was offended, accusing me of why I thought that I was better than him, while I did not think that at all. I stayed calm and respectful throughout the conversation. He continued constantly calling, pleading in his messages to "give him one more chance." "Another chance at what?" I was thinking. He is who he is, and he is not for me. It got to a point where he was reaching out to me through other sources also; it turned into harassment, and I got worried. Of course, my dear friend Joely volunteers for a Jewish civilian patrols organization, and this organization was able to put a stop to it once and for all.

I spoke to the *Shadchan* about him again and explained what had happened. I asked if she could look into future potentials a little deeper. I have children, and such incidents should not happen. This match she tried to make was based on him being an open-minded person and coming from such a wonderful family, which is indeed very nice, but the family is not the most important thing to me. The bond that a man has with his family, especially with his mother, I do find that to be crucial, but for the rest, it does not matter much. "It is not necessary to focus on the family so much; a *heimishe* but open-minded strong, grounded, well-rounded, true, chivalry and thorough gentleman is what I am looking for. Not only because he would have to be strong and confident to be with an unusual Jewish woman like me, but also because you would set a constant example for my sons."

The *shadchan* explained that I should not set my standards so high and be a little more open-minded in this situation. "In this situation?" In the "me being different" situation. In the "me being different mainly because I am black" situation.

Sometimes, I am just appalled by the discrimination and double standards all around me. We recently went through a war where a madman tried to wipe out our nation. Where blonde hair and blue eyes were praised and preferred, and the darker you were, the worse. Even though we went through this in the most negative possible way, I witnessed how this mindset is still way too often correlated within our own communities, still today. I witness how blonde hair and blue eyes are often considered to be nicer and better within our communities. Unfortunately, I witnessed how my blonde child has been favored and praised much more often than my oldest darker child. My blonde boy received most of the attention; he was looked at, smiled at, and stroked over his cheeks first at whichever Jewish occasion we were. His beauty was always noticed, mentioned, and talked about first. One of my very close Hasidic friends from upstate New York would always first observe if my blonde Moishe was still as blonde as he was the last time she saw him. She had dark hair before she shaved it off and dark eyes herself, and so did her husband. Clearly, to her surprise, her second daughter Fraide came out blonde, and she just adored and praised this one daughter. At a family wedding, she randomly whispered to her mother in Yiddish, "Mamie, you see how blonde my Fraide is?" It seemed more like an obsession she has for her blonde daughter, and I recognize this "liking blonde" from others in Moishe also. Some just cannot believe that he came out of the dark me.

One time I picked him up from school earlier because he had some sort of an appointment with his pediatrician if I remember correctly. He sat in his stroller crying his *tuches* off over some silly reason which I refused to entertain. I ignored him completely while walking with him through Borough park, on our way to his appointment. He had very blonde *Payes* (side curls), and his face was red from frustration. While I was walking with him and completely ignored him, I saw other Hasidim observing the scene with concerned looks on their faces, probably thinking that I was a babysitter "neglecting someone else's unhappy *'Yiddish kind'* (Jewish child)." Those concerned people, too, I ignored. Then all of a sudden, I noticed that some men started to follow me. I was excited about their disappointment when they would find out how ignorant they were when they realized that this blonde Jewish child was mine. I let them follow me, acting like I did not notice anything, wondering for how long they would follow me before one of them gathered the guts to say something to me.

At a certain moment, Moishe screams to me in Yiddish, "Mamie! Mamie! I want my pacifier!" while sitting backward in his stroller on his knees, looking at me and pulling my sweater furiously with one hand while holding onto the stroller with the other. As soon as they heard that, they swiftly turned around. The one across the street stood still for a moment to process what he just heard and make sure that what he heard was indeed what Moishe said, and then he, too, turned around and went his way. I was slightly laughing but wished that the blunder was made more clear-cut in their faces.

I wish for these silly and biased ideas to stop. "And why should I settle for less because I am different?" I asked the *Shadchan*. "Why don't you believe that I deserve the very best and the very best only? Why must I be more open-minded just because I am different?"

I was not born religious. There certainly has not ever been a positive Jewish role model for me throughout my childhood years, which would have influenced me to make the Jewish religion appealing to practice and to become religious, especially not anyone Hasidic. On the contrary. Most Hasidim were born Hasidic and lived a Hasidic lifestyle their entire lives. They are so attached to the idea of who they are that most would be afraid to let go because they would feel like they would lose themselves and along with themselves, their family, and the entire community. They did not choose this life. They were born this way, and it was expected of them to live this way.

I was raised way differently. I had the freedom to think for myself, to pursue what was in my heart, and even to get support from my friends and entire family in whatever I pursued. My mother believes that true love is true freedom and unconditional. My mother was not necessarily pursuing what she believed in how I should live my life, but more so, what I believed in myself. I chose this life, while I definitely did not have to, and could have just had a much easier, more comfortable life without judgment and still getting support from my family and friends.

Still, I chose this life.

Even though I like art, dance, and singing perhaps "a little too much," even though my wigs are perhaps considered to be "too long," even though I might be considered too expressive in being feminine, and even though I am an unapologetic strong independent mother, daughter, sister, (great) aunt, friend, teacher, speaker and last but not least: black woman

The Jewish Hasidic spirit continues to live within me.

Printed in Great Britain
by Amazon